Send Me

General Jim Vaught and the Genesis of Joint Special Operations

Written by Paul Gable and Bryan Vaught

Table of Contents

Acknowledgements

Special thanks to God for providing the vision to see this book through all the way to completion! We are also extremely grateful for all the photos and encouragement that were received from Aimee, Ben, Cathy, David, Debra, Florence, and Johnny Vaught. Finally, we appreciate the help with editing and reformatting from Stase Wells at the Marine Corps University Library.

Prologue
A Soldier's Soldier

And I heard the voice of the Lord saying,
"Whom shall I send, and who will go for us?"
Then I said, "Here am I! Send me."

The above quote from Isaiah 6:8 best describes the 38-year career of Lieutenant General James B. Vaught (USA ret.). From his first permanent duty assignment until retirement, Vaught frequently found himself in the position of being selected for some type of special assignment or mission. His attitude and answer were always the same: "We'll get it done."

The "We'll" in that statement was the key to Vaught's success. He never forgot the Army required teamwork from the most junior private to the most senior general. It is not an organization that can have one person going off and doing his own thing. Nobody succeeds alone.

Drafted out of college in the late stages of World War II, Vaught passed his induction physical on April 12, 1945, the same day that President Franklin D. Roosevelt died, and he entered the Army as a private. After completing basic training and infantry training, he applied and was accepted for Officer's Candidate School, earning a reserve commission as a second lieutenant in the Army of the United States on February 20, 1946, at the age of 19.

During his career, Vaught served in combat as a company commander in Korea and a battalion commander in Vietnam. In addition to his initial infantry training, Vaught also completed glider flight, paratrooper, and Ranger school at Fort Benning, Georgia and Army flight school for fixed wing and helicopters at Geary Air Force Base, Texas.

While on active duty, Vaught found time to complete his college studies earning a Bachelor's Degree from Georgia State University and a Master's Degree from George Washington University. He also successfully completed all the special military schools necessary for promotion including the Army Command and Staff College, the Armed Forces Staff College, and the National War College. He still proudly wears the pair of gold cuff links presented to him by General Lemnitzer, per school commandant Admiral Fitzhue Lee, for graduating as the number one student in his class from the National War College.

Among the numerous medals that graced the left breast of Vaught's uniform when he retired were two combat infantry badges, two silver stars, two bronze stars, a distinguished flying cross, and three Legion of Merit medals. Over the course of his Army career, Vaught had literally "been there" and "done that."

When asked which decoration meant the most to him, Vaught put his right hand next to his ear and snapped his fingers several times, imitating the sound of small weapons fire.

"If you haven't been in a position to know what that sound means, you haven't been in the real Army," he said. "The combat infantry badge stands above all others because it means you've been tested in combat over a period of time and passed the test."

Vaught and the men he commanded passed many tests during his long career. He looked for two traits in those men: courage and competence. Both come from the experience of having done something and knowing you can do it again, according to Vaught.

"With those two traits, a person develops a willingness to get the job done whatever it takes," Vaught said. "Those were the unique men I looked for when something out of the ordinary came up."

Using the term special operations to mean any mission outside the purview of normal Army doctrine, Vaught participated in various special operations-type missions during his career. The last of these, the Iranian hostage rescue mission of April 24, 1980, remains the most bittersweet moment of his career, but also was the most important for the development of the Army as it is today.

On November 4, 1979, several hundred Iranian students, fueled with Islamic fundamentalist passion and led by a small, hardcore nucleus inspired by Ayatollah Ruhollah Khomeini, broke through the gate and stormed over the walls surrounding the American Embassy in Tehran, Iran. They took the 66 Americans inside hostage.

Since overthrowing the government of Shah Mohammad Reza Pahlavi in late 1978, Khomeini, a Shia fundamentalist, had been Iran's spiritual and government leader. He had set about making Iran an Islamist utopia under Koranic Law. Khomeini preached that America was the "Great Satan" that had to be driven from Islamic lands. Shortly before the students took over the embassy, Khomeini had called on "all grade-school, university and theological students to increase their attacks against America."

News quickly reached the American government that the students who had invaded the U.S. Embassy compound were armed and had threatened some of the hostages at gunpoint while severely beating others. With 66 Americans in captivity in a foreign country, the Pentagon began looking for ways to rescue the hostages.

At that time, Vaught was a Major General serving at the Pentagon as the Director of Operations, Readiness, and Mobilization in the Office of the Deputy Chief of Staff Operations, Department of the Army. Chief of Staff of the Army General Edward "Shy" Meyer selected him to work for Chairman of the Joint Chiefs of Staff General David Jones (USAF) as the overall Joint Task Force Commander for the hostage rescue mission.

It was a testament to Vaught's distinguished Army career that he was selected to lead the mission. It was also one of the biggest challenges he ever faced. In fact, it could be said he was asked to perform the impossible.

The American military in general was still going through its post-Vietnam hangover. Special operations units that had been used for certain types of missions during that conflict had, by 1979, largely fallen out of favor with traditional military planners. Fortunately, the Army had not totally abandoned the idea of the need for a special operations force. It had moved forward, if somewhat reluctantly, with the establishment of Delta force.

Delta had passed its final readiness exercises at Fort Stewart, Georgia and been certified as an operational unit just hours before the hostages were taken on November 4, 1979. Much of Delta's operational training to that point relied on the force operating in a permissive, or at least neutral, environment where it would have the help of local authorities for support and information in achieving its mission.

"At the time, Delta was not trained, equipped, or disciplined to go into a contested area and operate," Vaught said.

Delta would serve as the Army's main contribution to the Joint Task Force. The mission, however, would require the force to go a thousand miles into hostile territory, into the middle of the capital city with millions of residents, free the hostages, and get out without becoming bogged down in a pitched battle. To make matters worse, there was no plan for such a joint task force command. All four services—Army, Air Force, Marines, and Navy—contributed their best personnel and service equipment to the mission, but retained command authority to themselves.

Nevertheless, over a period of five and one-half months, Vaught and his men from all four armed services gathered the necessary intelligence, put together a plan of operation, trained the various elements of the force, staged the units to their respective "jump off" points, and got the rescue force inside Iran to a location now known as Desert One. The mission had to be aborted at this point due to mechanical problems with the helicopters, which were provided by the Navy. The helicopters' role in the mission was to transport the rescue force from Desert One to the embassy and, after the hostages were freed, to fly the rescue force and former hostages to the extraction area at Manzariyeh where they were to be transloaded to C-141s and flown out of Iran. Vaught and Company "C" of the 1st Ranger Battalion were to provide security in the area while the transfer to the C-141s was being accomplished.

While the details of the planning, training, and the mission will be dealt with later in this book, events at Desert One were confusing. Vaught, back at the task force forward headquarters in Masirah, Egypt, initially believed the mission was able to go forward and radioed General Jones to that effect. Several minutes later, Vaught received communication from his commanders at Desert One that they would have to abort the mission because of problems with the helicopters that brought their operational number below the level the on-scene commanders believed was necessary to carry on.

"I was very disappointed because we had come so close and I believed we could continue to Tehran," Vaught said. "If I had been at Desert One, and maybe I should have been, I would have continued the mission. However, I wasn't willing to give that order from so far away, and felt I had to leave the final decision to continue or abort to the commanders on the scene."

Instead of going into Tehran with the hostage rescue force, Vaught had chosen to move to the extraction point at Manzariyeh to oversee the security of the area provided by the Ranger battalion.

"In my experience, it's when you're getting everybody loaded up and ready to go that major problems can occur and you can take the most casualties," Vaught said. "That's why I chose to be at the extraction point."

After returning to the United States, Vaught met with President Carter and a representative from the National Security Council.

"I told the president I apologized for failing to complete the mission," said Vaught. "He was very gracious and said we gave him our best shot, and he accepted full responsibility for the mission's failure."

Nevertheless, as always happens in the military when this type of high-profile mission fails to meet its ultimate goal, reasons and, often, scapegoats are sought. Members of the task force were called to testify at closed-door hearings of both the Senate and House Armed Services Committees whose stated intentions were to find out what went wrong with the mission. The results of the committee hearings were inconclusive.

Next, Admiral James Holloway, a retired Chief of Naval Operations, was put in charge of convening a special commission to study the mission and deliver a report of the findings. Vaught took issue with many of the members of the commission, especially Holloway, who he believed was looking to deflect criticism from the Navy's faulty helicopters and lay the blame for the mission failure elsewhere.

A feisty man with strong opinions, Vaught, after appearing before the commission, went to General Jones with an ultimatum.

"I told him the press was making inquiries and wanted a statement from me about the mission," said Vaught. "I told him I was willing to keep quiet and protect the people who screwed the mission up unless the commission went headhunting. If that happened, I would immediately resign my commission and hold a press conference on the steps of the Pentagon and tell the press who screwed this thing up with his name at the top of the list."

The final report of the commission went way wide of the mark in Vaught's opinion. It was conducted by a group of officers who had no familiarity with special operations. Specifically, Vaught was extremely upset that nowhere in the final report was there mention of the problems associated with the helicopters.

"The Navy sabotaged the mission, in my opinion," he said. "They gave us faulty helicopters, then, when the helicopters failed, they had the Admiral who bought the helicopters and with absolutely no experience in special operations put in the position of chairing the investigating committee to find out what went wrong."

However, two recommendations came out of the report that changed the structure of today's military. The first was for the establishment of a permanent, ready-to-go joint task force for hostage rescue and other sensitive missions. The second was for the establishment of a Special Operations advisory panel of qualified, high-ranking officers that would review and critique military readiness to respond to future crises.

In later life, Vaught would describe the mission as a "magnificent failure." It is better described as a magnificent attempt to achieve the impossible that nearly succeeded. The staff Vaught left behind would shortly become the first staff of the newly formed Joint Special Operations Command.

Vaught remained at the Pentagon for another fifteen months before receiving his third star and being transferred to Korea in September 1981 as Commander of the Combined Field Army Republic of Korea until he retired in January 1983.

As he reflected back on his career, the pride was evident in Vaught's voice when speaking of his many accomplishments. However, he still got emotional when speaking of the aftermath of the hostage rescue mission. Vaught said, in his opinion, there are four types of generals (or flag officers) in the military: the warriors, the bureaucrat managers, the politicians, and the incompetents. One look at his record tells you Vaught was of the warrior category. Listening to him speak of his career, you know Vaught has little respect or time for those who fit into one of the other three categories.

Vaught was always on the cutting edge of performance and led the way in integrating modern technology and development into military service including the use of jet skis, satellite communication, and night vision technology. After retirement, he continued to serve as a consultant to private defense contractors where he was involved with building the MH-47 and was often called on by the Army for advice.

The impact General James Vaught made on an international scale is immeasurable. In 1981, *The Washingtonian* magazine ranked him one of "Twenty Real Men" because "he fit the traditional image of masculinity: rugged, outspoken, commanding." This was not the first nor the last time Vaught was recognized for bravery, leadership, commitment, and devotion to his country. These traits, which took him far and influence a large part of American history over the last century, are due in large part to his Horry County, South Carolina roots.

"I had a very interesting career," Vaught said. "For a little old country boy from Horry County I did all right. My upbringing and my roots in Horry County enabled me and were a real foundation and motivator for all the things I was able to do throughout my career. I was very happy and pleased with what I had accomplished, and I left the Army with good feelings after thirty-eight years of service."

Chapter One

After emigrating from Hannover, Germany, the Vaught family came to Horry County, South Carolina through the port of Charleston in 1683. Peter Vaught secured a land grant of 8,000 acres from King Charles II of England. The land grant ran from the Atlantic Ocean, at the location of the present-day Dunes Golf and Beach Club, west to the Waccamaw River near the current Highway 90. The high ground along that route is still known to locals as Vaught Ridge, dating back to the original land grant.

Understanding the early history of Horry County is helpful in understanding the character of its native sons. Charleston was settled by a diverse group of people who established one of the most tolerant early societies in the English colonies.

"Charleston was an extremely tolerant city during colonial times, especially in the area of religion," said one local historian. "People who couldn't get along in other colonies often moved to Charleston to live."

However, not everyone was able to fit into Charleston society. In colonial times, Charleston established twelve outposts in a rough semi-circle radiating out from the city as a first line of defense against Indian and other attacks. King's Towne, later Kingston and now Conway, was one of those original outposts. It could be said, with tongue in cheek, that those who couldn't get along in other colonies went to Charleston and those who couldn't get along in Charleston settled the outposts.

Whether Peter Vaught fit into that description is lost to history, but he was among the early settlers of what is now Horry County. Today Horry County is best known for the East Coast resort city of Myrtle Beach. Millions of visitors arrive each year from the states east of the Mississippi to lie on the beaches, play golf, and enjoy the other attractions throughout the county. However, the Horry County of Peter Vaught's time was, for all intents and purposes, an island unto itself.

The area was essentially cut off from much of the rest of South Carolina by the water barriers of the Waccamaw and Pee Dee rivers. The only transportation network that tied Horry County together was the rivers, tributaries, and streams. Travel to the rest of the state was accomplished by boat until well into the 19th Century. Sitting in the coastal plain, much of the land was swamp and bogs. Inland, there was considerable sand mixed in the soil making even subsistence farming a difficult undertaking. Residents, especially the early settlers, had to be rugged individualists in order to survive. That individualism has continued to the present day. Horry County natives still take great pride in the county's nickname, "The Independent Republic."

The Vaught family established a salt works at the beach location as well as a blacksmith's shop, an oaken barrel production business, and a commercial fishing business throughout its holdings. The remains of the dipping vat for the barrels are still visible today behind the ninth green of the present Waterway Hills Golf Club off U.S. 17 just north of Myrtle Beach.

The Vaughts and their extended family took part in many of the early causes of the American colonies, including the Revolutionary War. Matthias Vaught, an ancestor of James, was a member of the Little River Regiment of the South Carolina militia that contributed to the defeat of a force of British Army regulars by Continental Army forces at the Battle of Cowpens in January 1781. The victory at Cowpens was a decisive moment in the Southern Campaign of the Revolutionary War that initiated the re-conquest of South Carolina from the British.

Francis Marion, another direct lineal ancestor of James Vaught, played an even bigger role for the Continental Army during the war. Known as the "Swamp Fox," Marion is credited as being the first American commander to consistently use special operations guerilla style warfare as his typical plan of attack. Marion and his men traveled on paths in the swamps, emerging to conduct surprise attacks on larger British forces and then quickly disappearing back into the swamps.

The British were successful in taking and garrisoning much of South Carolina, including Charleston with the help of Loyalist Tories, but were never able to garrison the Pee Dee region controlled by Marion's Williamsburg Militia. A combination of excellent intelligence and the ability to "live off the land," both important elements in special operations today, was the key to the success of Marion's militia. Peter Horry, for whom Horry County is named, served under Marion in the Williamsburg Militia.

Marion and his militia were successful in keeping a southern front open in the Revolutionary War tying up British troops that could have made the difference in the war had they been deployed against Washington's forces further north. An argument can certainly be made that Marion made as important a contribution to victory for the Americans in the Revolutionary War as any commander in the Patriot army.

James B. Vaught was born into this family on November 3, 1926 in the town of Conway, South Carolina, the county seat of Horry County. The son of John Marion Vaught, Sr. and Ruth Thompson Vaught, James was the fourth of eight children. When James was born in 1926, his father was a partner in a haberdashery located in Conway, South Carolina. After the 1929 stock market crash, the business followed the same path as much of the American economy: a consistent downward pattern.

John Vaught's partner, Austin Permenter died in 1931, automatically dissolving the partnership. After the liabilities of the business were settled and the assets divided up, Vaught was left with a total of $83 cash. The business was closed, and the Vaught family moved out of town to a small farm in the county that John was able to put a down payment on with his remaining money.

"We were self-sufficient on the farm so we didn't have to worry about having a roof over our head or food on the table," said Vaught. "We got along fairly well during the Depression, but there wasn't really any extra money."

At that time, schools in South Carolina ran from grades 1-11. The age for entering school was six, but Vaught's mother enrolled him in the Tilly Swamp School at the age of five.

"I had a brother one year older, but I was bigger than he was," Vaught said. "I could already read and write, so, when it was time for my brother to go to school, my mother took me along to the Tilly Swamp Grammar School and insisted I be enrolled also."

Vaught's youth consisted of school, church, and family activities, much as any child growing up on a family farm in rural America in the 1930s. Farm life required work from everyone in the family. Living in the "Bible Belt," the church not only served spiritual needs, but also much of the social needs of rural families. To this day, Sunday services and Wednesday church dinners are attended by most of the families in Horry County.

"From the time we could walk, we had chores to do around the farm," Vaught said. "The only two social centers we had were school and church. We really didn't go into town that much, and there wasn't much to do there when we did."

After spending seven years at the Tilly Swamp School, Vaught moved to Conway High School, which served grades 8 through 11. In addition to his studies, Vaught was involved in many extracurricular activities, the most important being the Conway Tiger football team. Weighing a solid 170 pounds by his final season, Vaught was the quarterback on offense and a linebacker on defense of a Conway team that went 7-1-1 and won a regional championship.

"There weren't a lot of substitutions in those years, so I played a full 48 minutes each game," Vaught said. "We had a pretty successful season, and I was known as "Mr. Tiger," a nickname that followed me to the Citadel in 1943."

Among his other Conway High activities was membership in the school's Calliopean Literary Society where he would meet Florence Epps, an event that would take on great importance for Vaught in later life.

Vaught applied to and was accepted by the Citadel, the South's answer to West Point. Even though World War II was raging at the time, it wasn't visions of a military career that entered into Vaught's decision to apply to the school.

"I wanted to be a doctor, and I would have been a good one," Vaught said. "Most people don't know it, but, at that time, nearly one-third of the graduates from the Citadel went on to become doctors. That's why I chose the school."

Vaught entered the Citadel in the fall of 1943, still two months shy of his seventeenth birthday and more than a year away from being eligible for the military draft. Although an honor student at Conway High School, Vaught experienced early struggles in his college math course. Already possessing a fierce determination to succeed, he sought out a tutor and put in extra hours in order to pass the course.

"I quickly realized that my math background was not as strong as that of most of the other students, but I saw that as a challenge to be overcome, not an excuse to fail," Vaught said.

He completed his freshman year with solid academic achievements and excelled at the military training required for all students at the Citadel. Vaught returned for the fall semester of his sophomore year, but soon the war would interfere with Vaught's plans of a medical career.

"In the fall and early winter of 1944, ten American divisions suffered considerable casualties in the Argonne Forest in Europe and in the islands of the Pacific," Vaught said. "The Army panicked and decided to draft college students. When I turned eighteen in November 1944, I knew my days as a college student were numbered."

Drafted early in 1945, the military student was about to embark on a military career that would stretch thirty-eight years. Although he didn't know it at the time, Vaught's plans to become a doctor were at an end. Instead he would go on to become one of the highest-ranking generals in the U.S. Army.

In April 1945, Camp Croft, South Carolina was booming with new recruits, one of which was Private James Vaught. Since early 1942, 65,000-75,000 draftees (called selectees) per year received basic and advanced infantry training there in preparation for joining a combat unit in the European or Pacific theaters. Camp Croft was an Infantry Replacement Training Center whose mission was to train soldiers as individual replacements and supplements to units already in the field. Initially these soldiers were known as fillers to help get units up to full strength in the beginning of the war and later as replacements for those lost to combat. The firing ranges at Croft consisted of pistol, rifle, machine gun, mortar, antiaircraft, and antitank ranges.

The course was nineteen weeks long and was designed first to turn a civilian into a soldier, and then provide that soldier with the skills necessary to survive his coming combat experiences. All the men received basic infantry skills. They were next split up to receive specific skills in preparation to joining a rifle, heavy weapons, cannon, anti-tank, headquarters, or service unit. The emphasis was on rifle companies where the most casualties were experienced with ten of the sixteen training battalions devoted to that mission.

During Vaught's training at Camp Croft, the war in Europe ended with the unconditional surrender of Germany on May 7, 1945. Shortly after Vaught completed basic training, Japan accepted the terms of surrender in the Potsdam Declaration of July 26, 1945. The Japanese government notified the U.S. government of that acceptance on August 19, 1945 with the official surrender documents signed in Tokyo Bay on the battleship *USS Missouri* on September 2, 1945.

With combat operations winding down in the Pacific and ended in Europe, Vaught applied for immediate entrance into Officer's Candidate School at Fort Benning, Georgia after completing his training at Camp Croft. The first step was to pass a preliminary OCS interview, which he did. To aid his application, Vaught called on General C.P. Summerall who was currently serving as the President of the Citadel and whom Vaught knew slightly from his three student semesters at the school. General Summerall wrote a letter of recommendation for Vaught urging the Army to immediately appoint him to OCS.

Vaught was accepted into the OCS program and transferred to Fort Benning to await the beginning of the next class of officer candidates. While waiting for the officer class to start, Vaught worked his way into a class at the airborne school, which was also located at Fort Benning. "I didn't want to waste the time, and I thought any extra training I received would help me later," Vaught said.

Vaught joined his OCS training class in October 1945 and was commissioned a second lieutenant in the Army of the United States on February 20, 1946 at the age of nineteen. In ten months, he had risen from the rank of private to the rank of 2nd lieutenant, at least in part because of his Citadel experience, but he was also on the bottom rung of the officer's ladder.

The Army has a hierarchical system for officers, which can play an important part in promotion. On the top rung are those who graduated from West Point and are immediately commissioned into the Regular Army. The middle rung is made up of graduates from Reserve Officers Training Corps (ROTC) courses, who are commissioned as reserve officers. The bottom rung is the OCS graduates who are also commissioned as reserve officers, but have generally not completed four years of military training like those graduating from West Point or ROTC courses. Most OCS graduates remain in the Army only for their initial commitment. Those who decide to make the Army a career need to convert to a Regular Army commission at some point in order to be competitive for promotion, but they still are generally looked on as second-class citizens when competing against West Pointers and ROTC Distinguished Military Graduates.

There have been exceptions, the most notable of which was General George C. Marshall who graduated from Virginia Military Institute and rose to the job of Chief of

Staff of the Army (the Army's top general) during World War II. After the war, Marshall went on to become Secretary of State and, later, Secretary of Defense, both in the Truman administration. However, the other top generals associated with World War II—Eisenhower, Bradley, Patton, and MacArthur—were all West Point graduates. Regardless of the type of commission he held, Vaught was on the way to Germany in early 1946.

Cadet Vaught at The Citadel in 1943

Chapter Two

Bamberg, Germany is a town in Bavaria located on the Regnitz river near where it joins the river Main. Bamberg was one of the few cities in Germany that suffered very little damage during World War II because an artillery factory was located near the town. The proximity of the factory and its anti-aircraft defenses kept Allied planes from making bombing runs on the town.

When Vaught arrived in Bamberg in the spring of 1946, the U.S. Army in Germany was now an army of occupation. A four-power Allied Control Council had been established on August 30, 1945 for the administration of Germany. Each of the four—France, Great Britain, the Soviet Union, and the U.S.—had a zone of occupation within Germany where the Commander-in-Chief of the respective forces issued commands and directives.

In reality, the administration of each zone of occupation lay with the forces within it. Initially, the American plan called for harsh treatment of the defeated Germans and strict non-fraternization between U.S. troops and German citizens. There was a general feeling among U.S. government officials and U.S. Army commanders that Germany had been treated too kindly after World War I, a condition that eventually led to the rise of Hitler and the Nazi Party taking over the German government and leading it into World War II. This time, it was felt the duty of American troops was to treat Germans with such sternness that they would be thoroughly degraded and never allowed to again threaten Europe with a general war. The initial plans called for Germany to be de-industrialized and reduced to a country of small farms, which could not support the rebuilding of a large military force.

The purpose of the Allied Control Council was to provide central administration over the country, but differences between the United States, Great Britain, and France on one side and the Soviet Union on the other led to the council's demise. It could not act except upon unanimous agreement of the four powers, which was difficult to achieve due to the Soviet Union acting in its own interests almost from the beginning of the occupation. Acting on orders by Soviet dictator Joseph Stalin from Moscow, the Soviet occupation forces effectively refused to work with the other three occupying powers in administering Germany. The ultimate goal of the Soviet Union was to force the United States, Great Britain, and France out of Germany, laying the entire country, and virtually all of Europe, at the feet of the Soviet Union. While the Soviet plan was not entirely successful, the Soviet representative to the council walked out on March 20, 1948, never to return, effectively ending the combined forces administration of post-war Germany by that body.

It was as early as July 1945 when American officials began to realize that the initial plans for Germany couldn't work because of the devastation that much of the country had suffered in the last six months of the war as well as the total disregard exhibited by the Soviets for any plans but their own. It was no longer a decision between an economic base of industry or agriculture, but one of keeping the German population from starving to death.

Upon his arrival in Bamberg in April 1946, Vaught was assigned as a platoon leader of the 820th Military Police Headquarters Company at Bamberg. His company was part of the recently established 32,000-man United States Constabulary force in Germany. It was in the process of being trained as the occupation and security force for all of the American Zone of Occupation in Germany and Austria. Its mission was to maintain general military and civil security in the zone and to back up the military government of various size detachments, which were present in all cities, towns, and villages of 5,000 or more persons throughout the U.S. Zone. Constabulary forces needed to know not only the traditional military duties of a soldier, but also police methods such as how to make arrests and deal with a foreign civilian population. When the Constabulary became operational on July 1, 1946, it took over from tactical forces that had occupied and policed the U.S. Zone since the end of the war in April 1945. The occupying forces maintained control, but they were incapable of performing the other necessary police functions because they were largely combat forces trained and equipped to fight and win the war. Hence, the Constabulary had inherited a large basket of thorny, deferred police functions.

"An early 1946 Washington decision caused me to be given the worst job I ever had during my thirty-eight years in the U.S. Army," Vaught said. "What caused this? The Army decided it would authorize officers and certain key senior non-commissioned officers to bring their families to Germany. This policy caused some very bad, long lasting public relations problems because there were no empty houses in which these families could reside."

"The Military Government decided to take possession of German houses in Bamberg to serve as housing for the families when they arrived," said Vaught. "I was one of the lieutenants ordered to serve the eviction notices on the German families living in the houses the Army was taking over. It was the worst job I ever had in the Army, but the Military Government had the authority to do it and I had orders to do the job."

Vaught, several enlisted MPs, and an interpreter went from house to house serving the eviction notices that gave the families only a few days to gather together their personal belongings before an Army truck would show up to move them out.

"They were allowed to take only clothes and personal items," Vaught said. "All the furnishings had to stay in the house. One man got so upset he set fire to his house."

The most difficulty was dealing with the widows of German soldiers killed in the war, according to Vaught.

"I remember one hausfrau whose husband was killed in the war," he said. "She started crying and wouldn't stop. She had lost her husband during the war and was now losing her home. I felt like crying too."

After a few weeks, the eviction was completed, and the homes were occupied by American families during the Spring and Summer of 1946. The Army tried to find other housing for the ousted German families; however, some wound up in displaced persons camps forced to live among persons who were abused by the Germans during the war.

Displaced persons (DPs) were the largest people problem in Germany for the first couple of years after the war ended. Estimates ranged from eleven million to as many as twenty million persons who were displaced in Europe because of the war. A majority of this number came from the concentration camps, forced labor camps, and prisoner of war camps that were freed by the Allied armies. In the American, British, and French zones of occupation, there were also DPs who had fled the advancing Soviet armies because of the stories of rape, pillage, and plunder accompanying the advances of the Soviet troops. DPs came from every country that had been invaded and occupied by the German army during the war. At the end of 1945, approximately 6,795,000 displaced persons were in the process of being cared for in the American, British, and French zones of occupation along with uncounted millions of Germans.

Those who were easily classified and willing to go back to their place of origin were generally gone from the DP camps by the time Vaught arrived in Europe. This left those whose classification was still a mystery or those who did not want to return to their country or area of origin, either because there was nothing to go back to or because they did not want to go back into an area occupied by the Soviets. In addition, many of the Jews wanted to go to the British Mandate in Palestine rather than return to their former country.

During its first six months, the Constabulary worked against suspected black market and subversive activities. It conducted "check and search" operations against both displaced persons camps and the German population. In the first six months, 2,681 black-market transactions and 173 subversive acts were uncovered by Constabulary operations. Another early mission of the Constabulary was to reorganize and develop the German police force. This allowed the Constabulary to leave the less important policing matters in the hands of the Germans so it could concentrate more on the apprehension of major criminals, black marketers, and other special operations of a more military nature.

Colonel Earl Wheeler, who had commanded the 350th Regimental Combat Team in the American Trust Zone since the war ended in April 1945, was now the G-3 Operations, Plans, and Training Officer of VI Corps, which had been selected to become the Headquarters of the U.S. Zone Constabulary. The 32,000-man force was split into three brigades of three regiments each and one separate regiment, which would have one squadron in Austria, one in Berlin, and one as a special operations, on-call squadron. The primary task of Major General Ernest N. Harmon, a crusty, foul-mouthed cavalryman who had dynamically commanded two different armored divisions in Patton's 3rd Army during the war, was to get the Constabulary organized, trained, and ready to take over the U.S. Army's job of U.S. Occupation Zone police and security on July 1, 1946 – a Trojan task to say the least.

In late April, about two weeks after Vaught and eleven other newly commissioned OCS second lieutenants had arrived in Bamberg, they were detailed as military police officers with instructions to take off their hard-earned crossed infantry rifles insignia and pin on the MP crossed pistols insignia. Vaught and three of the other second lieutenants were ordered to report to Colonel Wheeler.

Vaught and the other three newcomers were told by 1st Lieutenant Hugh Donovan, the 820th Executive Officer who was MP trained and the highly regarded former commander of the 820th, that Colonel Wheeler would select one of the four to be leader, organizer, and commander of a VIP Escort and traveling security force for General Harmon's train (formerly the personal train of high-ranking Nazi Herman Goering). The escort force would also serve as a riot control demonstration platoon when the Harmon train visited each squadron in the "getting ready" Constabulary.

"We reported to Colonel Wheeler at 0900 as directed," Vaught said. "All four of us were seated on chairs in front of Colonel Wheeler's desk. He was looking at our Form 66 Officer Qualification records. Suddenly he looked up and said 'Who is Vaught?'. I jumped up and said 'Lieutenant Vaught sir.' He said, 'Citadel, huh?' I said, 'Yes sir, a year and a half until I was drafted in April 1945. He said, 'Since you are Citadel trained you at least know how to shine your boots and be on time. You get the job. Don't get a big head over your selection. If you don't cut the mustard, one of the others will promptly replace you. Go down the hall and report to Lieutenant Colonel Creighton Abrams. He will tell you what we want you to do.'"

Abrams had commanded the 37th Tank Battalion, a unit in Patton's 3rd Army, from September 1943 until the end of the war. His battalion landed in Normandy in July 1944 and was in continuous action until the German surrender. One of his most noteworthy achievements was spearheading the relief of Bastogne during the Battle of the Bulge. Abrams was considered the most distinguished tank officer of his generation by no less an expert than General Patton himself. He went on to become Chief of Staff of the Army in July 1972. The M1A1 main battle tank in the U.S. Army bears his name today.

Wheeler was an infantry officer who served with the 63rd Infantry Division in Europe and later went on to become Chief of Staff of the Army from 1962-64 before being selected as Chairman of the Joint Chiefs of Staff from 1964-70.

"One of the unwritten requirements to reach the rank of general officer is to have a mentor or two along the way," said Vaught. "Abrams and Wheeler became my mentors at a very early stage of my career, and they helped me along the way for more than thirty years."

In Bavaria, there was concern among Army intelligence personnel that several thousand former SS troops were establishing a resistance movement hidden in the area around the Eagle's Nest, Hitler's mountain retreat in the Bavarian Alps above the town of Berchtesgaden. In late May, Vaught was ordered to take a small detachment of Constabulary troopers to the area and check out the rumors.

"The senior German Jagermeister (game warden) told us there was nothing to the rumors and guided us through the whole area including the Eagle's Nest itself, and there was nobody there," said Vaught. "There were hundreds of crayon scribbles all around the Eagle's Nest proclaiming that 'Kilroy was here', a slang term American GIs had scribbled everywhere they had conquered from Normandy to the Elbe River in Germany where the American and Soviet forces met in April 1945. Apparently there was no organized resistance and no will to fight left in the German people. All they wanted to do was rebuild their homeland and get back to some type of normal life."

After operating for six months in Bamberg, the Constabulary headquarters transferred to Heidelberg in December 1946, to take over the former headquarters of the 3rd Army, which was decommissioned and returned to the United States.

"All of the telephone communications in the American Zone in Germany passed through the former 3rd Army headquarters at Heidelberg," Vaught said. "When we got to Heidelberg, one of the jobs of the special troops was to oversee the operations of the telephone center."

After the move to Heidelberg was completed, the 820th Headquarters Company was reduced in size from more than 300 soldiers to seventy men with the rest being sent to other MP units in the American Zone. The unit was redesignated as a reduced strength company and would be used for Honor Guard, HQ security, and gate guard duty at the former 33rd Panzer Regiment Kaserne entrance gate.

Another interesting episode for Vaught involved German scientists who were still located at the Peenemünde rocket test and launch site, which was now in the Soviet Zone. Some of the top German rocket scientists had arranged to turn themselves over to the American forces near the end of the war, but more than 100 others were still at Peenemünde, caught up in the Russian occupation of eastern Germany.

While Vaught was on duty one afternoon in early 1947, as MP Officer of the Day at the main gate, two well-dressed men arrived asking to speak to the commander, claiming they were scientists who came from Peenemünde.

"They were obviously educated and well to do," said Vaught. "We listened to their story, which seemed believable."

Vaught then called Major Mederis, an ordinance intelligence officer who was in charge of collecting high interest information about the German rocket and atomic weapons development programs, which had been conducted for several years at a top-secret laboratory near Peenemünde. Two MPs escorted the men to Major Mederis' office.

They repeated their story to Mederis and claimed all of their associates wanted to come to the U.S. Zone to work for the Americans rather than worry about their future in the Soviet Zone. The major corroborated their story by checking with other Germans now working with him. Some had spent time at the Peenemünde lab and knew of these scientists. Higher Constabulary authority quickly approved Major Mederis' request to devise and conduct an operation to bring the remainder of the Peenemünde scientists out of the Soviet Zone. Vaught was selected to lead this mission.

"We told the two scientists who brought us the story that we would go on Saturday night to Peenemünde to collect their associates and bring them into the U.S. Zone," said Vaught. "We also told them that they were now under the protective custody of the U.S. Army and would be kept under guard until their associates were collected and brought out of the Soviet Zone. We told them one would have to go back with us and one would have to stay in Heidelberg. They seemed pleased and agreed to fully cooperate."

Saturday night, Vaught and the men chosen to accompany him to Peenemünde gathered equipment, cigarettes, and vodka and set off for Peenemünde. Vaught and his Constabulary troopers traveled in two jeeps, two one and one-half ton six-wheel weapons carrier trucks, and four two and one-half ton trucks for the evacuees. The group traveled approximately 150 miles to the location near Peenemünde where the German scientists were being held. The trip included going through five Soviet Army checkpoints manned by low-ranking Soviet soldiers who had been conscripted after the war and were not combat veterans.

"When we got to a checkpoint, our Russian speaking trooper would bribe the Soviet soldiers on duty with cigarettes and vodka and ask them to let us through," Vaught said. "This early in 1947, the forces weren't organized very well in any of the zones, and we had no problem getting through." He added, "Once we got to the location, we set up the weapons carriers to cover against any surprises and gave the scientists one hour to get together one suitcase and other personal items in hand and get on the trucks."

The return journey was uneventful. Vaught said one of the checkpoints had the same men on duty that they had seen on the way over. By now they were feeling the effects of the vodka and almost fell over raising the gate. The mission resulted in bringing out nearly 100 more scientists, most of whom soon wound up working on the U.S. Space Program at Huntsville, Alabama and elsewhere.

As a company commander of the 820th, Vaught reported directly to Lieutenant Colonel Abrams who gave him additional duties including overseeing the General Officer's Mess, the Officer's Mess, the motor pool, maintenance, and the WACs running the telephone center, as well as serving as prosecutor when necessary.

"I wound up with about 2,000 people working for me including civilians," Vaught said. "The secret was Colonel Abrams gave me an experienced master sergeant for every different assignment who ran the day-to-day operations. I basically spent my day going from unit to unit to sign necessary papers and check on how things were going."

His job performance combined with the reputation and experience of the officers he was working for provided Vaught with career-enhancing opportunities both immediately and later. While mentors are rising to the very top ranks in the Army, those they like are remembered and provided with special opportunities along the way. Vaught also made some opportunities of his own as he organized and acted as both player and coach of a football team that went on to win the Theater championship in the fall of 1947.

Shortly after winning the theater championship, Vaught was sent back to the United States on a temporary duty assignment to learn how to fly gliders. Gliders had been used in World War II as a means of putting infantry troops into enemy territory. Probably their most effective use was during the D-Day invasion when they were used as a complement to parachute drops to get infantry troops behind the German front lines.

"For the most part, gliders put more men on target ready to fight with less casualties than paratroop drops," Vaught said. "However, when the Air Force was split from the Army into a separate service, it said it would no longer support gliders."

Vaught and eight other junior officers were selected to go to Fort Benning to learn how to fly gliders since the Air Force refused to supply pilots. Vaught and the other officers successfully completed glider training and earned their "glider wings," but the problem was not solved.

"The Air Force would not supply planes to tow the gliders, so they still couldn't be used in an operation and gliders effectively left the scene," Vaught said.

Returning to Germany after the short hiatus in the States, Vaught was soon preparing for another move of the Constabulary Headquarters. After a year in Heidelberg, the 820th headquarters was moved again when USEUCOM (U.S. European Command) decided to take over the Heidelberg facilities. This time the destination was Stuttgart. As the unit was completing its move, Vaught received a letter from the Citadel and gave very grave consideration to leaving the Army.

"The Citadel football coach contacted me and offered me a scholarship to come back to the school," Vaught said. "My two-year commitment as an officer was up, and I put in my papers to get out of the Army and go back to working to be a doctor."

Colonel C. Gardner Gross, who had been a prisoner of war in the Pacific during World War II and to whom Vaught was then reporting, intercepted the papers and called Vaught in for a conference. He asked Vaught if he had heard about competitive tours that were being offered to gain a Regular Army commission.

"I told him I heard about them, but I wasn't really shot in the ass with the Army," Vaught said. "I wasn't a college grad, and I felt if I stayed in I would get every shit detail that came along while the ring knockers (West Point grads) would get the good assignments."

Colonel Gross told Vaught to think about it and come back the next day. Vaught also got some urging toward completing the competitive tour from Aimee Beers, the adopted daughter of an Army colonel, whom he had been dating for a period of time. Colonel Beers had served in the Rainbow Division with General Douglas MacArthur during World War I, so Aimee was very familiar with Army life.

"We talked about it, and she encouraged me to complete the competitive tour and then make up my mind about a career in the Army," Vaught said. Vaught went back the next day to discuss the competitive tour with Colonel Gross and found a surprise waiting for him.

"When I got back, he had filled out all the papers for me," Vaught said. "He told me the Army needed officers like me and told me to sign on the dotted line."

Vaught was re-assigned to the 26th Infantry Regiment in June 1948 for the one-year competitive tour with the infantry. The 26th, under the command of Brigadier General "Hanging" Sam Williams, had gone into Normandy with the first invasion force and later served as guards of the high-ranking German officials during their trials at Nuremburg.

"They were a bunch of tough hombres who had seen a lot of action," Vaught said. While he completed the four cycles in the competitive tour, Vaught also found time, at the direction of Williams, to coach and play quarterback for another Theater championship football team. He was commissioned into the Regular Army with the permanent rank of second lieutenant, even though he wore the rank of first lieutenant to which he had been promoted while still a reserve officer. The Regular Army date of rank was January 1, 1948, because you had to be twenty-one years old to be an officer in the Regular Army.

After Vaught decided to compete for a Regular Army commission, he and Aimee got married on July 31, 1948 in Germany. They delayed their honeymoon until completion of the tour. When it came, in the summer of 1949, the couple traveled through France to visit some of the battlefields from World War II. It was an eye-opening experience for Vaught.

"I wanted to visit some of the battlefields from World War II, especially Normandy," he said. "The thing that surprised me the most was the French didn't seem to have made any progress rebuilding their country since the end of the war. Many of the battlefields we visited looked like the battle had ended the day before." Soon orders came through for Vaught to return to the United States as a company commander in the 511th Airborne Infantry Regiment of the 11th Airborne Division.

Lieutenant Vaught in Germany 1946

Chapter Three

The U.S. Army, which Vaught had decided to remain in, was in the midst of major changes by the time he received his Regular Army commission. Historically, neither the U.S. government nor its citizens have supported the concept of a large standing army, except in a time of war, and they only want to fight wars with specific goals and objectives.

"The fact is the majority of American citizens don't like the military, and they don't like long wars. This nation was founded by people who wanted to leave behind the European tradition of kings, aristocrats, and standing armies that resulted in things such as the Hundred Years War between France and England," Vaught said.

In colonial times, the colonies used a militia system for local defense. When the Revolutionary War started, these local militias formed the first Continental Army units. The states each sent a prescribed number of troops to the Continental Army and sometimes resorted to drafting men for militia duty, but the federal government did not have the authority to conscript men into military service.

National conscription (the draft) was used for the first time during the Civil War, but the vast majority of troops on both sides were volunteers. The U.S. Army reached a troop strength of 2.1 million men during the Civil War with only approximately 2% being draftees. When both the Union and Confederate armies tried to draft men into service, massive resistance, sometimes violent, resulted.

The Conscription Act of 1917 was passed just months before the United States entered World War I, but the draft was unpopular in many areas of the country with many activists against conscription being jailed for obstructing recruitment or enlistment service. Even when conscripts entered the Army, many wound up being court-martialed for offenses such as refusing to wear the uniform, bear arms, or perform the basic duties subject to military authority.

The Selective Service and Training Act of 1940 established the first peacetime draft in U.S. history and, with war already raging in both Europe and the Pacific, the Army began drafting men in late 1940. Initially a cap of 900,000 men in training or limited military service was set, but as the needs of World War II increased, all men age 18-45 became subject to immediate conscription for the duration of the war plus six months.

In the 1930s, the total strength of the Army, which included the infant Army Air Corps, was just over 100,000 men. By early 1942, this number had increased to over one million with six infantry and two armor divisions. When the war in Europe ended in May 1945, the Army alone had over eight million men under arms with forty-eight infantry, sixteen armor and four airborne divisions manned. The Army Air Corps, Navy, and Marine Corps pushed this total to over ten million men in the service.

Immediately after Germany surrendered, Army troops were being detailed to go to the Pacific, but with the surrender of Japan in August 1945, the drawdown in troop strength began. By 1949, Army strength was again down under one million men, with many of its ten remaining divisions undermanned and lacking equipment. This major drawdown in strength was in full force even though the draft remained in effect and what would become known as the Cold War was becoming colder by the day. So, Vaught was in the Regular Army that was returning to its traditional role of the institutional

Army where training, planning, and changes to military doctrine were day-to-day duties, but the ability to fight a war was minimal.

"The regular Army, the U.S. Army, does not win wars. It only provides the foundations of planning and doctrine and a small permanent cadre of professional soldiers upon which to build in time of war. It is the Army of the United States, which includes the Regular Army, its reserve units, and the National Guard units and draftees called up in time of war, that wins wars," Vaught said with the experience of thirty-eight years in the system.

To make matters worse for the Army in 1949, the nuclear bombs dropped on Hiroshima and Nagasaki to end the war with Japan were having an effect on military doctrine. The Strategic Air Command was formed on March 21, 1946, under the command of General George C. Kenney as the Army Air Forces were beginning the reorganization and transition into the soon to be independent U.S. Air Force. SAC's mission was to provide a long-range bombing capability anywhere in the world. By 1948, the Joint Chiefs of Staff had a Joint Emergency War Plan codenamed "HALFMOON," which placed heavy emphasis on an atomic air offensive. HALFMOON called for dropping fifty atomic bombs on twenty cities in the Soviet Union within several days of the outbreak of war with that country. In general, the thinking at the time was that the Strategic Air Command and the atomic bomb were supposed to insure military supremacy for the United States. As long as they were adequately funded and supplied, nothing else in the military establishment much mattered.

Initially, President Harry Truman rejected HALFMOON and called for a non-nuclear alternative plan. However, when the Soviet Union blocked railway and road access from the western occupation zones in Germany to western forces in Berlin on June 24, 1948, Truman's thinking began to change.

This Berlin Blockade, as it became known, lasted for nearly a year and was one of the first major international crises of the Cold War. Total control of Berlin, split between the United States, Great Britain, France, and the Soviet Union since the end of the war and approximately 135 miles into the Soviet zone of occupied Germany, was a major goal of the Soviet government. The Soviet Union thought the blockade would make it impossible for the western nations to supply Berlin and that they would be forced to allow Soviet forces to supply the city, thereby giving the Soviet Union effective control over all of Berlin. However, the U.S. Air Force, British Royal Air Force, and air forces from other British Commonwealth nations formed the Berlin Airlift that flew over 200,000 flights and provided 13,000 tons of food daily to Berlin, effectively breaking the blockade, which ended in May 1949.

Into the midst of the blockade strode Lieutenant General Curtis LeMay in October 1948, when he assumed command of the Strategic Air Command. LeMay immediately attempted to unilaterally form American nuclear strategy by having SAC planners draw up Emergency War Plan 1-49, which upped the ante of a nuclear strike on the Soviet Union to 133 nuclear bombs dropped on a total of seventy Soviet cities within thirty days of the outbreak of war. LeMay also increased the SAC's independence by refusing to submit SAC war plans for review, a view the Joint Chiefs ultimately came to accept. For the next decade, the doctrine of massive nuclear retaliation would be the professed U.S. response to Soviet aggression with the Air Force and later the Navy's nuclear submarine force, gaining the major portion of U.S. military expenditures.

It was an Army significantly reduced in size and strategic scope in which Vaught was now a junior officer. After he returned to the United States, Vaught had time to attend jump school again. While he had already gone through this training prior to attending OCS three years before, he had never served with an airborne unit and did not make the number of jumps necessary to keep his certification.

"I wanted to draw jump pay, which was $110 per month at the time," he said. "I was only making $220 a month as a first lieutenant, so this was a 50% pay increase for me."

In November 1949, Vaught reported to the 11th Airborne at Fort Campbell, Kentucky to serve as a company commander in the 511th Airborne Infantry Regiment. Upon reporting to the 511th Regiment Commanding Officer Lieutenant Colonel Ben Harrell, Vaught received advice that guided him for the rest of his career.

"Colonel Harrell told me that I needed a man to manage my career. He told me to assume command of the man I see in the mirror every morning, keep him straight, and everything else will fall in line. It was excellent advice, and I never forgot it," Vaught said.

The 11th Airborne was a training unit at the time, but it was under strength and didn't have enough men to conduct effective training. In addition, the men were not taking the training jumps very seriously. Vaught was assigned the collateral duty of Regimental Safety Officer with the responsibility of reducing the number of accidents the regiment was experiencing from training jumps. Within two months, the number of training accidents the regiment experienced was reduced by 50% and at the end of four months, the number of training accidents had been reduced to virtually zero.

For his effectiveness in significantly reducing the number of training accidents, Vaught was made Regimental Adjutant, normally a major's job, when the position came open in March 1950. As adjutant, Vaught worked closely with the commanding officer seeing to the day-to-day affairs of the regiment. Three months later the Korean War broke out, and the training now took on more serious ramifications as men were being prepared to quickly go into combat.

Korea, occupied by Japan for thirty-five years until the end of World War II, had been split into two zones of administration at the end of the war, under the U.S.-Soviet Joint Commission. The Soviet Union occupied the northern half of the country down to the 38th parallel, and the United States occupied the southern half of Korea below the 38th parallel. Both the United States and the Soviet Union approved Korean-led governments in their respective halves. The Korean War resulted after both the North Korean and South Korean governments made attempts to take over governing the entire Korean Peninsula. In the early morning hours of June 25, 1950, the North Korean Army crossed the 38th parallel into South Korea supported by a heavy artillery barrage.

The North Koreans attacked with 231,000 troops supported by 274 tanks, 150 fighters, 110 attack bombers, and 200 artillery pieces. To counter this attack, the South Korean Army had 65,000 combat soldiers. Soon, the South Korean Army was in full retreat and suffering from mass defections in some units. The North Korean plan was to force a quick surrender by the South Korean government, thereby obtaining reunification of the Korean Peninsula under its control.

The United States had no real combat presence in South Korea when the war began, but on June 27th President Truman, under the auspices of U.N. Security Council Resolution 83, ordered combat forces to be moved from Japan to South Korea to support the South Korean government against North Korean aggression. However, it took time to move the American forces from Japan, and their initial entry into the war failed to stop the North Koreans. By September, the South Korean forces and their allies held only 10% of the Korean Peninsula.

American air power, both ground-based Air Force bombers from Japan and Navy carrier-launched planes moved to destroy the North Korean supply lines. This saved the day and allowed the buildup of reinforcements for South Korea-UN forces' counterattacks. Combined with an invasion by the 1st Marine Division far behind the North Korean lines, the coalition forces successfully drove the North Koreans out of South Korea and pursued them beyond the 38th parallel into North Korea. The coalition forces drove deep into North Korea before the Chinese entered the war to support the North Koreans.

The tide turned again with the addition of Chinese Army units into the war, and the coalition forces were driven out of North Korea with the North Korean and Chinese forces again entering South Korea. The UN and South Korean forces blunted a series of Chinese offensives, and slowly the coalition forces returned to the 38th parallel. By July 1951, a stalemate developed between the two sides approximately along the 38th parallel. Over the next two years, more bloody battles would be fought as the North Koreans and Chinese forces tried to gain a series of strategically important hills along the front lines. It was into this phase of the conflict that Vaught went to Korea.

Ordered to the position of company commander of a heavy mortar company with the 34th Infantry Regiment of the 24th Infantry Division, Vaught and his unit were trained in Japan for approximately six weeks before being shipped to Korea in February 1952. He was also promoted to captain during this time. Initially assigned to guard a theater ammunition depot, Vaught said the biggest threat to his unit was from the South Korean Army in May and June 1952.

"The South Koreans were not happy with the ongoing armistice talks and wanted to again take the offensive," said Vaught. "They tried to move units into the ammunition depot we were guarding, and we had to threaten them in order to get them to change their thinking."

Moved to the front lines, Vaught and his unit saw action against Chinese forces before the truce was signed in July 1953. He was awarded his first Combat Infantry Badge for his service under fire during the Korean War.

"I was involved in a lot of little things as the truce talks were going on. The lines between the coalition forces and the North Koreans and Chinese were not straight. They included salients at different points along the line, which both sides tried to straighten out before the armistice, and hills that were considered strategic by both sides. Attacks and defense on these types of positions were the type of action I saw in Korea," Vaught said.

The truce took effect at 10 a.m. with Vaught's unit at the front line along the Demilitarized Zone (DMZ). Vaught's unit was ordered to move back to Pusan by noon where it would be involved in the guarding of prisoners of war until prisoner exchanges were completed.

"We got five days to set up camp in a rice paddy. The first thing we did was build wooden platforms above the paddy so the area in which the tents were set up would be dry. One thing I learned early in my career was 'when you move into any area, you fix it up like you're going to be there the rest of your life.' This is what I tried to do during my career. That approach goes a long way to establishing good morale in the unit," Vaught said.

Vaught's unit was located at Prisoner of War Camp 2 in an old Japanese Army compound. It was assigned to guard women prisoners of war from the Chinese Army.

"That was the meanest, nastiest group I have ever been associated with, much worse than the men prisoners," Vaught said. "On the day they were supposed to be exchanged, we put them on a train with new cars. In no time, they wrecked the cars, breaking windows and tearing up the seats. We marched them off the train and back to camp and told their leader anymore incidents and they would wait a long time before they went home."

At the end of October 1953, the port area of Pusan caught fire because of ruptures in oil lines used to offload fuel from ships. A total of forty acres of houses burned with approximately 10,000 people losing their homes. Vaught and his regimental combat team were ordered to stop the fire, clean up the embers, and build a tent city to shelter 10,000 civilians displaced by the fire. Vaught organized a production line to build wooden frames for tent housing to house the homeless until more permanent housing could be rebuilt.

"As the operations officer of the 34th, I organized a provisional fire-fighting team that stopped the fire in four hours," Vaught said. "The next day, with the help of the 3rd Engineer battalion, we established a tent building production line, which put 10,000 Koreans into warm shelter in less than ten days."

This operation led to a personal commendation for Vaught from General Maxwell Taylor, Commander of U.S. and allied forces in Korea. He was commended for "exceptional performance and organizational skill" in stopping the fire and building the temporary tent shelters.

From December 1953 to February 1954, Vaught and the 34th Regiment were ordered to an area near Panmunjom at the DMZ with the mission to be prepared to accept 18,000 Chinese POWs who refused to return to China and were being sent to the island of Formosa (Taiwan) instead.

"On January 18-19, 1954, we received up to 1,000 POWs per hour," said Vaught. "We used a total of 541 two and one-half ton trucks to move the POWs to a holding area at the port city of Inchon and load them on ten specially configured LSTs, which would take them to Formosa."

The operation was completed during extremely harsh Korean winter conditions with no loss of life and only one "minor" truck accident. For his performance in this operation, Vaught received a personal commendation from Lieutenant General John Hull, Commander in Chief of the Far East Command.

In March 1954, Vaught returned to Japan where he served as Assistant Operations Officer at Camp Drake in Tokyo, Japan. He was involved in the planning for the return of four divisions, which would return to Japan from Korea during 1954-55. May 1954 saw Vaught receive orders to return to the United States where he would attend the ten-month Infantry Officer Career Course.

Captain Vaught and Aimee in Tokyo ~1954

Chapter Four

Vaught returned to the United States with eight years of active duty behind him. The remainder of the 1950s would be a time of education, training, and preparation. He was already being noticed by senior officers for his ability to accomplish tasks with considerable personal initiative, and he had successfully passed his first test of combat in Korea. Vaught was an infantry officer who was about to become even more familiar with the specialized tasks of that combat arm.

Vaught was assigned to Fort Benning where he attended the Infantry Officer's Career Course and Ranger school. The Infantry Officer's Career Course is one of the tickets that have to be punched by a career infantry officer while he holds the rank of captain. It focuses on combined arms warfare at the tactical level with realistic and difficult training in various environments. The career course is designed to increase the skills of a combat leader while teaching him how to think under combat conditions.

It was during the career infantry course that Vaught teamed up with several other captains in discussion sessions about the needs of the Army and the relative minimal funding it was receiving compared to the other military services.

"The Army was getting 18% of the defense budget at the time, even though it had the largest number of personnel. Even worse, only about one-third of the needed equipment replacements were even being worked on, and most of those were in the research and development phase. The Army was stocked with a bunch of junk left over from World War II and Korea. We started talking about it and throwing ideas around," Vaught said.

U.S. Military doctrine was still concentrated around the concepts of nuclear weapons and strategic bombing, even though this strategy had proved to be badly flawed during the Korean War. After the Chinese entered the Korean War and forced the U.N. forces into a retreat into the extreme southern portion of South Korea, the Joint Chiefs could not decide on a target or targets to be subjected to a nuclear attack that would change the course of the ground war in Korea. The possibility of a nuclear attack was discussed, then discarded, demonstrating the difficulties of the U.S. strategy, which planned for strategic bombing only with essentially no consideration of tactical fighting with conventional arms.

U.S. Allies, especially Britain and France counseled against use of nuclear weapons in Korea. They feared such action would bring an all-out war between the U.S. and China resulting in a significant change in U.S. commitments to NATO and Chinese encouragement of the Soviet Union to attack into western Europe. The British and French feared the Soviets would be able to extend their occupation to all of Europe at little cost because the bulk of U.S. military assets would be tied up in an Asian war.

In the first significant military action involving U.S. troops since World War II and with the United States still having a monopoly on nuclear weapons, the use of these weapons did not occur in Korea because of faults in the strategy. However, the Air Force and Navy successfully continued to push for increased funding to build up the stock of nuclear weapons and associated bombers and missiles.

To complicate matters even more after the Korean War, the Eisenhower administration developed a doctrine that the foundation of military strength was economic strength and the foundation of economic strength was a balanced budget. This put more strains on the defense budget and, since the cost of preparation for conventional (non-nuclear) warfare was more than that of building nuclear weapons, and the reliance on massive nuclear retaliation remained as the cornerstone of American defense policy.

"We can't afford to fight limited wars," said Secretary of Defense Charles Wilson. "We can only afford to fight a big war and, if there is one, that [nuclear] is the type it will be."

The Air Force had developed this policy in 1948 and contracted with industries in a large number of states to support the air power and nuclear doctrine. This gave the Air Force the greatest voice in Congress since defense contractors in many states filled its orders. The Navy, in the process of developing nuclear submarines and missiles, joined the Air Force in this argument. So, the Army and Marines remained on the fringes of defense spending, making do with antiquated weapons.

"The Army still had an 1898 model water-cooled machine gun that was obsolete by the time World War I was over, but it was still around and counted in the inventory," Vaught said. "There were a total of 105 different weapons systems in the Army, including stuff from both world wars. Most were obsolete and incompatible with each other."

However, Vaught and his comrades were not content to just talk about the modern weapons needs of the Army. They decided to develop Project MAN (Modern Army Needs). The group itself was a collection of up-and-coming junior officers. In addition to Vaught, it included Edwin "Shy" Meyer who would go on to become Chief of Staff of the Army, Herb McChrystal who spent his career in Army Intelligence before retiring as a major general, and George Casey, Sr. who went on to become a major general commanding the 1st Cavalry Division when he was killed in a helicopter crash in Vietnam. Vaught briefed his class group on the project, and all agreed to help.

They chose ten weapons and other pieces of equipment that needed replacement. Information about the original cost and cost to modernize was collected. After they had collected all the information, the group laid the equipment out on a field at the school complete with visual aids such as charts and graphs and briefing documents about each piece. In addition, they made recommendations about acquisition and the cost of replacements. One other recommendation was that the makeup of the Army should include over 50% of its troop strength in the three combat arms – infantry, armor, and artillery.

"At that time, 37% of the Army's manpower was in the combat arms with 63% in support units," Vaught said. "We felt those percentages should be reversed if the Army was to be successful with its primary mission, which is to fight and win wars."

The initial briefing on Project MAN was presented to the Commanding Officer of the Infantry School. He supported the project and arranged for further briefings. In total, five briefings were given up the chain of command with the final briefing including the Secretary of the Army and members of Congress.

"It was a beginning," said Vaught. "We got some things approved in the next budget, but it would take ten years before we saw real changes in weapons systems and equipment."

After completing the career officer's course, Vaught attended Ranger school. The school's curriculum is an extremely intense leadership-training course, considered to be the Army's premier leadership course. Today it is considered a necessary step that must be taken by career officers. The course concentrates on small unit operations for which the Rangers have been known since their inception during World War II. Students typically spend twenty hours per day in training and average four hours per day of sleep, all while living on one or two meals per day, sometimes less. The typical student loses twenty to forty pounds during training.

In addition to standards for pushups, sit-ups, and pull-ups, students must be able to complete a five-mile run in forty minutes or less during the initial Ranger assessment tests. Water survival and confidence, combination night/day navigation with a map and compass, terrain runs, obstacle courses, hand-to-hand combat, weapons training, demolition, airborne refresher training, and a timed 12-mile forced march with full gear were all included in the initial phase of two weeks at Fort Benning. From there, the students went to Florida for three weeks of training in the swamps and the ocean with a total of four patrols that increased in intensity and difficulty as the course progressed. The final phase was mountaineering, which included basic climbing skills and three more patrols.

The patrols are conducted under simulated combat conditions, which means little sleep, little food, and almost no shelter. Basically, the only shelter the men had were the ponchos in their rucksacks. The rucksacks weighed approximately seventy pounds, which, after being hauled around for twenty to twenty-one hours per day felt three times as heavy and made the small of the back ache constantly.

Students are graded by instructors on their demonstrated leadership abilities in various positions in various situations. Equally important are the peer reviews where the students grade each other. Vaught graduated number one in his Ranger class and remained at the school as an instructor for two more cycles of Ranger candidates while awaiting orders.

"It's a very intense course, and when I went through the attitude seemed to be they wanted to kick you out rather than have you succeed," Vaught said. "Things have changed now. The school is just as difficult, but there are opportunities to repeat phases and succeed now where students would have failed before. I have always believed in a policy of encouragement to try to help soldiers who, for any number of reasons, may not be ready to succeed on their first try. Most times you can turn things around for the soldier, and you have a much better Army as a result."

After completing the student training and earning his Ranger designation, Vaught moved to a teacher position as he served as the S-3 Operations Officer for the summer Reserve Officers Training Program (ROTC) camp for the Military District of Atlanta.

"We had 2,200 ROTC cadets that we phased through summer training in three battalions," Vaught said. "The S-3 is responsible for staffing the summer camp as well as the scheduling and support necessary to get the various units of cadets to where they belong each day."

At the end of the camp, Colonel Johnson Lemmon, ROTC Camp Commander, said, "This has been my third ROTC Summer Camp and it has been the best run, thanks largely to the performance of Captain James Vaught."

When summer camp was completed, Vaught spent the first semester of the new school year with a Jr. ROTC program in the Atlanta Public High School System. He also went back to college to work on completing a bachelor's degree that he had begun in 1944.

"Now that I was on a career track in the Army, I knew I needed to complete my bachelor's degree and probably a master's in order to be competitive for higher rank," Vaught said.

In May 1956, he was off to Geary Air Force Base in Texas to attend Army Flight School. The Army had essentially been out of the aviation business since the Air Force became an independent service in 1948. The original mission of Army aviation had been forward observance for artillery to help adjust fire and bring it in on the enemy, as well as a means to deliver messages between units in the field. Later, air support of ground troops had been introduced into Army aviation doctrine, but by the end of World War II, strategic bombing of enemy supply lines and industries had become the main mission. By the mid-1950s it was determined that some of the original mission requirements of Army aviation remained, and new doctrine was looking at getting more combat arms on an aviation basis for more rapid deployment, so the Army began training a small number of pilots from its officer ranks.

"We had to train at an air force base because the Army had no facilities to train pilots," Vaught said. "We were trained in small, fixed-wing aircraft that could act as artillery observers and also provide some support for the troops on the ground. I believe to this day that slow-moving, fixed-wing aircraft is the best way to provide fire support for the infantry."

Vaught's pilot training was one of the bumpier experiences in his career, but it also brought out the determination and grittiness that became hallmarks of his Army career.

"I was born with a color vision deficiency--not enough to disqualify me for pilot training, but one that sometimes can affect my depth perception, especially as it gets dark," Vaught said. "Because of that deficiency, I am not a great pilot. I had some hard landings, but I managed to get through the school and earn my wings."

After completing flight training, Vaught was assigned to the 325th Airborne Infantry Regiment, a component of the 82nd Airborne Division at Fort Bragg, North Carolina. A glider infantry regiment during World War II, the 325th Regiment had been converted to parachutes by the time Vaught arrived.

"There was lots of debate in the Army about the usefulness of airborne units at the time," Vaught said. "The big debate centered around how airborne units could defend against enemy armor while establishing one or more airheads and expanding outward from them."

Projects were undertaken to establish combat plans if the Army needed to fly paratroops to places such as Israel, Korea, and the Philippines to help support local troops in the area. Israel had just fought its second war in eight years against the neighboring Arab countries, and more wars looked a likely possibility in the future. South Korea still faced a much larger force across the border in North Korea and had to be on almost constant alert for another attack from that country. The Philippines was the home of two large U.S. military installations, Clark Air Force Base and Subic Bay Naval Base, but the country was made up of almost 7,000 islands, some of which had large contingents of indigenous communist sympathizers.

"The Army and the other services are constantly updating combat plans for many countries based on possible threats and current conditions," said Vaught. "None of this means the U.S. is planning to go to war, but the plans and preparations are kept up to date just in case. The thinking was that paratroops would be the first force into these and possibly some other countries to establish initial U.S. presence. How to make those units successful in their mission was the purpose of the plans."

At the time, the only artillery piece the airborne forces had to combat tanks was the SPAT. Each airborne regiment had one SPAT platoon of four pieces each assigned to it. The SPAT was a tracked, four-inch gun, which had to be towed into position by six men. Once the piece was in position, the wheels were collapsed horizontally and sand bags were placed on each wheel to attempt to keep the piece from jumping around each time it was fired. The maximum range was 2,000 meters with the effective range only about half of that.

"It was an unbelievably ineffective piece of weaponry," said Vaught. "If a tank gets to within 1,000 meters you're in big trouble anyway and, even if the gunnery on the tank is terrible, it takes only about two shots to zero in on the location. So the doctrine was the SPAT would be towed into place, fire off a couple rounds, and have to move again. It was really no defense at all for the regiment."

Vaught, with the concurrence of his regimental commanding officer Colonel Charles M. Gettys, started working on a replacement for the SPAT. At the same time, Lieutenant General Jim Gavin was appointed head of Research and Development for the Army.

Gavin had been in the Army since 1924, when he first enlisted in the Army. He successfully competed for an appointment to West Point and earned his commission in 1929. After West Point, Gavin studied at the U.S. Army Infantry School at Fort Benning. Colonel George C. Marshall headed the infantry school at that time, and Major Joe Stilwell was head of the tactics department. Gavin developed his own style of leadership based on Stilwell's teaching that you should not ask your soldiers to do anything you were not prepared to do yourself.

In 1936, while stationed in the Philippines, Gavin became concerned about the Army garrison of 20,000 troops' ability to successfully defend against attacks by the Japanese if such should occur. Gavin moved back to West Point to work in the Tactics faculty in 1939 while the German forces were in the initial stages of their Blitzkreig into Poland. It was during this time that Gavin first became enamored by the possibilities of airborne forces that could be inserted into areas in large numbers ready to fight the enemy.

Gavin was transferred to Fort Benning where he completed jump school in August 1941. He assumed command of the Company C of the newly established 503rd Parachute Infantry Battalion. He was later moved to Operations and Training officer (S-3) of the Provisional Airborne Group, where he developed combat tactics and doctrine for airborne troops.

Gavin's rise during World War II was nothing short of meteoric. Constantly working on airborne training, tactics, and doctrine, Gavin developed much of the airborne doctrine for World War II. As a colonel, Gavin led the 505th Parachute Infantry Regiment into battle during the invasion of Sicily. This action marked the first time the U.S. Army had ever conducted a regimental size parachute drop. By D-Day, Gavin was a Brigadier General and assistant division commander of the 82nd Airborne Division. He led Force A in a night parachute drop of three regiments onto the Normandy Peninsula. By September 1944, Gavin was the youngest major general in the history of the Army and was commanding the 82nd Airborne Division. He led the division on a jump into Holland as the Allied forces were driving to Germany.

After the war, Gavin continued developing new doctrine for airborne troops and by the time he was head of R&D, Gavin was proposing an airborne cavalry regiment consisting of lightweight armored vehicles and helicopters.

While Gavin and Secretary of the Army William Bruckner were visiting the 325th Airborne Infantry Regiment, the old soldier met a relatively new one (Vaught) who was also one to "think out of the box" where doctrine and tactics were concerned.

"We took everything we had to fire at tanks—bazookas, grenade launchers, howitzers, and the SPAT—to the range to put on a demonstration for Secretary Bruckner," said Vaught. "None of it worked very well, and the SPAT was funny to watch as it was jumping around with each shot and being manually towed from one position to another."

The demonstration proved that airborne troops were still inadequately supplied to counteract attacks by armor against them. Vaught had been working on an idea that only his regimental commander was aware of at the time. It consisted of a 106 mm gun atop a light armored vehicle, which would operate as part of a mechanized battalion with airborne regiments.

"I gave a presentation based on charts and renderings of what this would look like," Vaught said. "General Gavin bought into the idea immediately, and Secretary Bruckner said, 'Do it.'"

Twenty-two months from the time of the presentation, the first prototype of what would become known as the Sheridan fighting vehicle rolled off the assembly line.

Captain Vaught in Georgia ~1956

Chapter Five

Vaught's education continued as he was chosen to be the leader of a group of ten officers and forty-four enlisted men from the 325th Regiment that were sent to Frenchman's Flat, Nevada to be observers of an atomic test as part of Operation Plumbbob. Operation Plumbbob consisted of twenty-nine mostly atmospheric atomic explosions—the largest, longest, and most controversial atomic test series in the United States. Many of Plumbbob's explosions were tests for warheads on intercontinental and intermediate range ballistic missiles, but they also included smaller air defense and anti-submarine tests as well as tested the effects on military and civilian structures, radiation and bio-medical studies, and aircraft structure tests.

Men were sent from all branches of the service so the military could begin to determine how the average soldier would stand up both physically and psychologically to the rigors of a nuclear battlefield. On June 24, 1957, Vaught's group observed test shot "Priscilla," which was a high-altitude balloon shot, a simulation of an atomic bomb being dropped on the battlefield. The group was in an open trench less than 3 miles from "Ground Zero" when the 37-kiloton atomic device (the third largest atomic yield in the series) was detonated. Each man wore a REM badge to determine how much radiation exposure he experienced during the test.

"It was an unforgettable experience," said Vaught. "Once you see one of those explode, you know you never want to see another one."

After the Frenchman's Flat experience, Vaught reported to Fort Leavenworth to attend the Army's Command and General Staff College. The Command and General Staff College is the lead agency for the Army's leader development program, and its classes are designed to advance the art and science of the profession of arms in support of Army operational requirements. In a class of 600 officers, Vaught was the only one to have witnessed an atomic detonation.

When Vaught arrived at Fort Leavenworth, the Army was undergoing a change in its operational requirements. America's defense policy still planned for massive retaliation in the event of Soviet aggression despite the lessons provided by Korea that conventional warfare was still very much a possibility for America's armed forces. The French defeat in Indochina (Vietnam) at Dien Bien Phu in 1954 and Chinese shelling of the Nationalist Chinese-controlled islands of Quemoy and Matsu in the same year demonstrated that all of Southeast Asia contained potential trouble spots for conventional conflict, and America was a signatory of the Southeast Asia Treaty Organization (SEATO). The chance of nuclear war erupting in any of these spots was minimal. The Suez Crisis of 1956 that included the second war between Israel and its Arab neighbors demonstrated that the Middle East, with its increasingly important oil reserves, was another potential trouble spot for conventional warfare.

Nevertheless, the thinking in the Eisenhower administration had not changed since the Korean War ended. Believing that the conflict in Korea was an aberration and that conventional American combat forces would not again be deployed to fight communist armies in either Asia or Europe, Secretary of State John Foster Dulles enumerated what would become basic American defense theory for the remainder of the 1950s.

"The basic decision was to depend primarily upon a great capacity to retaliate, instantly, by means and at places of our choosing. Now the Department of Defense and the Joint Chiefs of Staff can shape our military establishment to fit what is our policy, instead of having to try to be ready to meet the enemy's many choices. That permits of a selection of military means instead of a multiplication of means. As a result, it is now possible to get, and share, more basic security at less cost," Dulles said.

Dulles' statement reiterated the concept of massive retaliation, which had been put forth by the Air Force and Navy since 1948 and also reflected the Eisenhower administration's desire to reduce military spending and work toward a balanced federal budget. At the end of the Korean War, the Army had 1.5 million men under arms, but a reduction in force of approximately 600,000 men was planned for the remainder of the 1950s. This number was reached late in the decade when the Army's manpower strength was again at approximately 900,000.

"The Army of the late 1950s really wasn't very good," said Vaught. "Most of our divisions were under-strength and the overall quality of the soldiers was, frankly, lacking."

The policy of massive retaliation and reduced army strength was not without its detractors. General Matthew Ridgway, commander of the 82nd Airborne Division and 18th Airborne Corps during World War II, the general credited with turning the Korean War around after the Chinese entered combat operations and who succeeded Eisenhower as Supreme Allied Commander Europe for the NATO forces, fought the concept.

Ridgway believed air power and nuclear bombs did not reduce the need for powerful, mobile ground forces that could seize territory and control populations. Ridgway was concerned that the policy of the Eisenhower administration to reduce the size of the Army would leave it in a position where it was unable to counter the growing Soviet military threat. As Chief of Staff of the Army, Ridgway had recurring disagreements with the administration until he retired on June 30, 1955.

Replacing Ridgway as Chief of Staff was Maxwell Taylor, another World War II paratroop general. Taylor agreed with Ridgway's assessment of massive nuclear retaliation as the primary U.S. defense policy. He considered the Eisenhower administration's "New Look" defense policy as dangerously over-reliant on nuclear arms and neglectful of conventional forces.

Taylor believed that small, conventional wars could break out from unchecked local aggression or error. The Army had to be able to stop such small wars as well as conduct a major war on the nuclear battlefield.

Taylor moved to change the structure of the army division to acclimate it to the potential demands and dangers of the nuclear battlefield while also attempting to obtain the Army additional funding from the defense budget. He developed the concept of the Pentomic Division, which essentially eliminated battalions and regiments from the structure and replaced them with battle groups in what was a system of "5s". Each division was composed of five battle groups, each commanded by a colonel. Each battle group consisted of five infantry rifle companies, a combat support company, and a headquarters company. Each company was commanded by a captain, leaving majors and lieutenant colonels out of the direct command structure, and a long time (from captain to colonel) between commands.

The expansion of the Army budget would come from the inclusion of nuclear weapons as part of the standard firepower of the new Pentomic division. Pentomic division artillery originally included the Honest John, a surface-to-surface rocket carried on a mobile truck platform with a nuclear warhead. Later, the Davy Crockett, a nuclear projectile launched from either a 120 mm or 155 mm recoilless rifle was included in the Pentomic division arsenal for use against Soviet troop formations in Europe. The inclusion of nuclear weapons would help the Army get a bigger slice of the defense budget. "Nuclear weapons were the going thing and, by including some in the division armament, the Army staked out its claim to a share of the nuclear arsenal," Taylor later wrote in his book *Swords and Plowshares*.[1]

Taylor gave the opening address to Vaught's class, telling the students this would be the first class at the Command and General Staff College to receive instruction on the Pentomic Division concept. Taylor gave the college staff six weeks to re-write lesson plans that would concentrate on the Pentomic concept.

The instruction during those six weeks would include administration, supply, and personnel. There would also be an intensive five weeks on atomic warfare and how to determine the size of the weapons needed in various situations.

"One of the highlights of the year was how the Army interfered with Christmas leave," Vaught said. "Traditionally there was a two-week leave during which the students took off to all parts of the U.S. On Friday, Dec. 17th, the day before leave was supposed to start, we found out there would be a 2,000-4,000-word paper due the day we came back from leave. That meant everyone would have to stick around over Christmas and use the library facilities to complete the paper rather than having two free weeks. There was a lot of grumbling in a lot of families that night."

The ironic part of the assignment was that it was supposed to be on an original idea to improve the combat capability of the Army, preferably associated with atomic weapons. The grades given out on any assignment at the college were A, B, C, or U for unsatisfactory. When the grades came back to the class, over 79% of the students received a grade of "U." A board was convened to determine why the grades were so poor.

"I had received a B minus with a comment that said there was not enough documented research in the paper," Vaught said. "When I appeared before the board, I asked how you could include documented research on an original idea. The board threw out all of the results, so the whole exercise was a waste of time that ruined Christmas for most of the class. As anybody who spent any time in the service will understand, that was a perfect example of the 'Army way.'"

Another paper Vaught wrote during his year in Command and General Staff College had much more far-reaching consequences. In switching to the Pentomic Division, the question of replacements into the smaller units while maintaining combat readiness had to be addressed. He developed a concept of changing the way two-year draftees or three-year voluntary enlistees were trained. The Army was still drafting men each year as the threat of the Soviet Army marching into Western Europe was ever-present in military thinking.

Vaught recommended taking the draftees directly into a Battle Group and performing basic and advanced training at that level rather than in separate locations as had been the case. There was precedent for this going back to the Civil War, and it was really only during World War II and, later, Vietnam that basic and advanced training was conducted before a draftee or volunteer was sent to a regular unit.

---

[1] Maxwell D. Taylor, *Swords and Plowshares: A Memoir* (Da Capo Press, 1990), 171.

"We had a draftee for two years, and it seemed to me the best use of that time was to send him directly to a Battle Group where basic, advanced, and unit training would be conducted over the first ten months of his enlistment. After thirty days of leave, he could then be sent to Korea or Europe with his unit when it deployed," Vaught said.

Vaught submitted his paper at Fort Leavenworth, and it worked its way up the chain of command, eventually reaching the Department of the Army in Washington, D.C. where it was turned into an Army Regulation entitled "Pentomic Unit Replacement System." The concept was for unit replacement rather than man-for-man replacement bringing a more highly trained, cohesive force to replace one already in the field. This was not the concept used in Vietnam where draftees and volunteers were thrown piecemeal into units in the field to replace wounded or end-of-tour personnel. However, it is standard practice in the Army today, allowing a soldier to remain with the same unit throughout his time in the service. It is known as the U.S. Army Home Station and Unit Replacement Policy.

From Command and General Staff College, Vaught was ordered to 3rd Army Headquarters at Fort McPherson, Georgia. This was an opportune assignment as it allowed him to go to night school at Georgia State University to complete his bachelor's degree in Business Administration, finally putting him on a level playing field educationally with other Regular Army officers.

He was initially assigned to the job of director of officer personnel assignments for the 3rd Army, a lieutenant colonel's job he was filling as a captain. The 3rd Army included all the units and forts in the Old South.

"It had the largest number of troops of the six army districts in the U.S., approximately 90,000, and it was not manned at full strength," said Vaught. "My first task was to do a complete assessment of the resources and the qualifications of the officers for the jobs they were holding."

He continued, "After six weeks, I determined the resources were badly out of balance, especially in the G-2 (intelligence) area. Almost without exception, those officers holding down the G-2 spots were either castoffs from other areas, especially operations, or within one year of retirement and most had not been to any type of intelligence school. With rare exceptions, across the broad spectrum of the Army, the wealth and talent should be spread equally among all areas."

Intelligence officers assigned to operational units had never been a priority of the Army. Even during World War II, much of the intelligence gathering was conducted by the Office of Strategic Services (OSS), which was established by a military executive order from President Franklin D. Roosevelt issued June 13, 1942. Prior to this, the Army and Navy had code-breaking sections that competed with each other and did not share information.

When Roosevelt established the OSS, he requested that General William J. "Wild Bill" Donovan, a World War I veteran and Medal of Honor recipient, draft the plan for the intelligence service. The United States did not have an intelligence service at the time, and the State Department had eliminated its code-breaking section in 1929 when Secretary of State Henry Stimson ordered it to shut down because "gentlemen did not read other gentlemen's mail."

The OSS, however, operated on a national level collecting and analyzing strategic information required by the Joint Chiefs of Staff and conducting other operations not assigned to other agencies. However, it never had jurisdiction over all foreign intelligence activities or intelligence activities that would provide information to units in the field. Immediately after the war, President Truman dissolved the OSS, and its functions were split between the State Department and the War Department. When Truman signed the National Security Act of 1947, establishing the Central Intelligence Agency, the United States had for the first time a permanent peacetime intelligence agency. Most of the former OSS functions were taken up by the CIA after its formation.

"During World War II, we had so many men in the service that through talent and inclination provided the services with excellent intelligence officers at the various unit levels," Vaught said. "After the war, most of these men left the service, and intelligence at the unit level became an afterthought."

Vaught, however, believed that good intelligence was one of the key elements of successful military operations. He put together a plan to improve the intelligence capabilities throughout the 3rd Army and briefed 3rd Army commander General Clark Ruffner on it. Vaught's plan called for approximately 300 intel-qualified officers to be placed with units throughout the 3rd Army. Ruffner approved the plan and sent Vaught to Washington, D.C. to meet with personnel detailers.

"They liked the idea in Washington, and an intelligence school was started for personnel who would specialize in the intelligence field," Vaught said. "Within one year of the plan being adopted, we had about 60% of the intelligence billets manned by competent people, which was a major improvement."

Vaught moved from the officer personnel assignment to a similar one dealing with enlisted personnel. "The overall plan was to get qualified personnel into jobs where they wanted to be so they could do something both for the Army and for themselves," he said.

Vaught took the final exam for the last course he needed to complete his bachelor's degree requirements on a Friday night with orders already in hand to report to Fort Benning on Monday morning as the Commanding Officer, Headquarters Company, 1st Battle Group, 11th Infantry Division.

"The last course I needed was Money and Banking, and our professor was a very demanding one. We started with twenty-six people in the course and had seven on the night of the final. I needed the course to graduate but had doubts I would pass it up to the end. About a week after I got to Fort Benning my wife called me to tell me I had gotten an "A" in the course, so everything worked out fine and I had my degree," Vaught said.

When he arrived at Fort Benning, Vaught got the opportunity to put the theory from his Battle Group training paper at Command and General Staff College into practice. Working for Colonel George Patterson, Commanding Officer of the 1st Battle Group, Vaught wrote the Overseas Replacement (OVREP) plan for replacing units in Korea.

Assigned to command the Headquarters Company, 1st Battle Group, 11th Infantry Division at Fort Benning, it was Vaught's job to prepare the Battle Group for deployment, as a unit, to Korea. The first six months of his assignment included overseeing the training of the battle group as well as the many logistics preparations needed for deployment.

Vaught was promoted to major, while still commanding the headquarters company, after fourteen years of commissioned service. This rather late promotion time was due to an antiquated promotion system used in the Army at that time.

"Officers like me could be promoted in the Army of the United States only one grade above their permanent rank in the Regular Army," Vaught said. "I had just been promoted to the Regular Army rank of captain, so I was finally eligible for promotion to major in the Army of the United States. Both General Taylor and General Hull tried to get the Army to waive the requirement in 1953 and get me promoted to major, but they were denied."

As the time neared for deployment to Korea in early 1961, Vaught went to Korea as part of the advance party to prepare facilities.

"This was the first time a replacement unit was sent intact to Korea," said Vaught. "Korea was always at the outer edge of Army planning. Since the end of the Korean War, the thinking in the Army was that the troops in Korea would be coming home next month, so the divisions were generally under strength and the facilities way below standard."

Below standard was exactly what he found on his first inspection of facilities that would be available for the Battle Group.

"We were going to be attached to the 7th Division, and the facilities they had available for us were only about 50% of our needs and everything was way below standards," Vaught said. "It was the damnedest mess you ever saw."

The training and capabilities of the troops in Korea were also not up to standard in Vaught's opinion.

"I was invited to view an Army Field Test of one of the units in place on the DMZ," he said. "It was a sorry mess. If the unit I observed was in actual combat, it would have killed more of its own soldiers than the enemy's."

After making his thoughts known to the commanders on the scene, Vaught was challenged to produce better. He made an offer to have the 1st Battle Group come off the ships transporting it to Korea and board trains to the DMZ where it would immediately go into the field and take a three-day field forces test.

"They didn't think we could pull it off, but we had trained to a very high standard while at Fort Benning," Vaught said. "Because of the unit replacement concept, we had soldiers who knew and were used to each other and also knew the job they were supposed to perform."

The Battle Group arrived at the DMZ at night, dug in with parapets and aiming stakes in place, and camouflaged the entire area. The next day it conducted a defensive drill, repelling an enemy attack in the training area, and followed that performance with a display of its offensive capabilities.

"The chief umpire of the exercise gave us a score of 99 out of 100 for the field test," Vaught said. "We had proved what training and the unit replacement concept could accomplish."

During the analysis of the exercise, Colonel Patterson credited Vaught with putting together the plan that had gotten the Battle Group into such a high state of readiness during training. As a result, he was re-assigned by General Carter B. Magruder, Commanding Officer of the United Nations and U.S. Forces in Korea, to the position of a staff officer assigned to G-1, 8th Army Headquarters in Seoul.

"I had known General Magruder during the occupation of Europe, so we went back a long ways," Vaught said. "I was essentially a trouble shooter for 8th Army HQ, going out to different units, observing their state of readiness and helping, where necessary, to establish training plans to improve their readiness."

Vaught remained with 8th Army HQ until May 1962 when he rotated back to the United States to attend Armed Forces Staff College in Norfolk, Virginia.

"In February 1962, I learned that I had been selected to attend the next class at the Armed Forces Staff College in Norfolk, VA," Vaught said. "The class was to begin in September 1962. My friends in the Infantry Branch devised a way for me to return to the U.S. in May."

Operation Plumb Bob "Priscilla" Nuclear Blast in 1957

Chapter Six

Vaught attended the five-month course at the Armed Forces Staff College in Norfolk, Virginia from September 1962 through February 1963. The curriculum is designed to provide students with an opportunity to experience all of the planning and operational challenges a staff officer could anticipate over a three-year joint duty assignment, whether the assignment is on the Joint Staff, a Joint Task Force, or a Service Component Staff. It consists of four areas: Administration, Strategy, Campaigning, and the Joint Planning Process.

"When you were selected for the Armed Forces Staff College, it was almost assured you would be selected to attend the War College in the future," said Vaught.

Vaught's faculty advisor for his fifteen-person work group was Colonel Chuck Wright, who had been operations officer for the 26th Infantry Regiment when Vaught had been assigned to it in 1948-49.

"The five months I was at the Armed Forces Staff College were most enjoyable," said Vaught. "Colonel Wright asked me to help teach the other members of our work group—who were all Air Force, Marine, and Navy officers—how to do joint staff work."

Vaught's work group earned the best work group citation at the class graduation in February 1963.

Initially scheduled to become the operations officer of the newly forming 11th Air Assault Division, Vaught was reassigned to go to the Pentagon five days before completing the Staff College course.

"I really wanted to go to the 11th Air Assault because it was an experimental unit working on new tactics," Vaught said.

The 11th Air Assault was formed at Fort Benning, Georgia on February 11, 1963, combining light infantry with helicopter transport and air support. According to some Army reports, the initial tests of the 11th Air Assault, in the context of conventional warfare, did not go well. Nevertheless, Secretary of Defense Robert McNamara and the new Army Chief of Staff General Earle Wheeler pushed through the concept. The 11th Air Assault was soon merged with the 2nd Infantry Division. The combined unit was reflagged as the 11th Air Assault Division. Its ground-based fighting units were mainly infantry. These soldiers would now move by vertical takeoff and landing aircraft, normally helicopters, to seize and hold key terrain on the battlefield and to directly engage and destroy enemy forces. The 11th Air Assault Division would be re-designated the 1st Air Cavalry Division when it arrived in An Khe, Vietnam in late August 1965. Vaught would become a battalion commander in the 1st Air Cavalry Division during his first Vietnam tour in 1967-68.

When he arrived at the Pentagon, Vaught went to work for Lieutenant General Ben Harrell, who was Assistant Chief of Staff for the Force Development Department of the Army. Vaught was assigned as Chief of Infantry Doctrine in the Doctrine and Concepts Division of the Army staff. The Army was undergoing somewhat of a resurgence from the 1950s when it took a distinct back seat to the Navy and the Air Force in budget and strategic importance. Shortly after John F. Kennedy took the oath of office as President of the United States, he learned that he had very little flexibility with a potential military response in the wake of crises. The Pentagon's preferred doctrine of massive nuclear response did not work at all with the smaller, more localized type of guerrilla conflicts that were occurring in Latin America, Africa, and Asia.

Kennedy wanted flexibility in a potential response to these types of conflicts with the ability to quickly send 10,000-20,000 troops to potential flashpoints that threatened American interests in order to attempt to control a situation before it erupted into a larger conflict. As a result, the Army was beginning to think in terms of mobile, flexible response tactics while still preparing for the big European War against Soviet forces that some in the Pentagon still believed would happen. Vaught's job was to study these new types of potential conflicts and provide new infantry doctrine and weapons systems to fight them.

"My first job, in early 1963, was to get rid of the Davy Crockett," said Vaught. "General Abrams called me in and said 'I know you know how to bust through the bureaucracy here and get things done.'"

The Davy Crockett was a nuclear artillery weapons system from which a small, sub-kiloton warhead could be launched from a 102 mm recoilless rifle launcher. The range of the weapon was approximately 1.25 miles. The Davy Crockett was manned by members of the Davy Crockett platoon, which was a part of the Atomic Battle Group Headquarters Company, stationed every few kilometers, to guard against attack by Soviet forces. The concept was that in the event of an attack on West Germany by the Soviet Army, the nuclear shells would be fired to incapacitate, slow, and kill Soviet forces. The radiation from the shell exploding would make the area in which it landed uninhabitable for approximately forty-eight hours, a timeframe that would be used to bring larger NATO forces to the battle area to stop any Soviet advance. Theoretically this weapon would give infantry units the ability to destroy large tank or infantry formations on the front line of the advance. However, the accuracy wasn't very good, especially when the Davy Crockett was employed against moving targets, such as tank formations.

Additionally, the Davy Crockett platoons required security clearances because they were handling nuclear weapons. When the Davy Crockett was first deployed, each unit in the Battle Group was tasked with providing men for the new platoon, which would man the weapon system. A lieutenant, generally highly rated in his evaluations and trained on the Davy Crockett, would be assigned as the new platoon leader, but the men in the platoon would come from existing personnel in the Battle Group.

Tradition in the military, which could also be called an unwritten law, holds when your unit is tasked with providing a man for transfer to another unit, you get rid of the worst man in your unit, thereby making him someone else's problem. Consequently, the new Davy Crockett platoons were largely made up of soldiers who had been determined to be "screw-ups" in their former units. When a readiness inspection was conducted on the Davy Crockett platoons, inevitably they were found deficient because of security clearance and other personnel problems, and the lieutenant in charge of the platoon was replaced for failing to have the platoon at the required state of readiness.

"We were losing a lot of good lieutenants because they were responsible for the manning and training of these new platoons while the men assigned to them could not qualify for a security clearance due to past records from their former units," said Vaught. "General Abrams gave me six weeks to get rid of the Davy Crockett system, and we got the job done although we ruffled some feathers along the way."

Purchasing or cancelling a weapons system for the Pentagon is not a simple process. Each system is part of the budget process, proposed by the executive branch and approved by Congress. Each system has its champions in the Pentagon, in the administration, and in Congress, as well as the contractor who produces it. It can be much more of a political game than a decision based on need, logic, and common sense. If you're not careful, a decision can be overridden or ignored by the change resistance—essentially the bureaucracy comprised of civil servants with permanent jobs in the Pentagon.

Another project involved a very promising and accurate missile system, which could propel an atomic warhead 440 kilometers. This missile system had been developed at Redstone Arsenal. Fort Sill's Artillery Center had developed the doctrine for this new system, which was named the Pershing Quick Reaction System (QRA). The QRA system would be forward deployed near the front lines in East Germany to deter attacks by the Soviet Army.

The Pershing would be used if the Soviet Army launched an all-out attack on Germany, or a missile strike on the U.S. homeland. The QRA would then be used in a retaliatory attack against Soviet forces massed for the attack or into the Russian homeland. The original system did not have enough range to reach Moscow, but engineers at Redstone Arsenal and Fort Sill found a way to extend the missile's range from 440 miles to 660 miles, enough to reach all the way from Germany to Moscow, if needed.

By extending the range of the missile so it could impact Moscow, the system became one of deterrence. Because of their proximity in Germany, Pershing missiles could be used in a retaliatory attack against the Soviet capital before missiles launched at the United States would reach their destination.

The initial deployment called for three squads of three missile batteries each. They would rotate among 147 surveyed firing positions with no battery staying in one firing position for more than three days.

"The Russians had spies in West Germany around all the troop positions and bases," Vaught said. "The movement of the missiles every three days made sure the Russians could not get a fix on any of the positions, even from spies on the ground, before they moved again. This caused the Soviet Army considerable problems because the Pershing was both a tactical and strategic weapons system that they could not neutralize or knock out."

On November 10, 1963, artillery Lieutenant Colonel Pat Powers, armor Major John McHenry, and Vaught were tasked to prepare an urgent request for an appropriation of $25 million to enable the extension potential. Over the next eleven days, the group worked long hours to finish the request. They had worked through the night of Thursday, November 21, 1963, polishing up a presentation for President Kennedy on extending the range. The presentation was to be made to the president on Saturday, November 23rd after he had returned from a political trip to Texas.

"We decided to have lunch together at a small place near the Pentagon on Friday," said Vaught. "We had just sat down when the news came across the television that the president had been assassinated. After things settled down, we wound up making the presentation and recommendation to President Johnson who agreed with us and gave the order to extend the range of the Pershing missile to 660 miles so that its range could be extended to hit Moscow, if necessary."

Another larger project was the arsenal study, which looked at every weapons system the Army currently had and recommended what the Army would need for weapons for the five-year period 1965-1970. At the time, there were 105 different, direct-fire weapons systems in the Army inventory, including water cooled machine guns used in World War I. There were fifteen different types of machine guns, seven different mortars, and other duplication up and down the line of Army weapons.

Vaught was named the study director by General Harrell. The final product was called the Army Requirement for Direct Fire Weapons Systems (ARDFIRE) 1965-1970, which is catalogued in the Army Library at the Pentagon.

"General Wheeler and General Harrell gave approval to bring fifty officers to Fort Leavenworth to work on the study for 120 days," said Vaught. "Over the course of several months, we developed seven different combat scenarios to determine what weapons systems would be needed in each."

The study group made use of simulated short and medium range moving map scenarios with the best intel estimates of potential enemy confrontations in jungles, on the plains of Europe, and in the deserts of the Middle East.

Bi-weekly briefings were used to report progress and problems. The goal was to complete the study in 110 days, brief it to a staff of general officers, make necessary changes, finalize the product for briefing to General Wheeler on the 118th day, make any further changes, and publish the study on the 120th day. All goals were met with the final seven-volume product measuring fourteen inches in height.

After General Wheeler signed the two-page Executive Summary, the report was briefed to all Army major commands, the House and Senate, and the Army Material Forces Command. The Material Command was responsible for implementing the material changes, and the Continental Army Command was tasked to implement necessary doctrinal changes.

"The study made 105 recommendations of which 103 were approved," Vaught said. "We wound up reducing the number of weapons systems to twenty-six. In summary, the product saved the Army billions of dollars and facilitated procurement of direct fire weapons used in the Vietnam War through Desert Storm."

In May 1964, General Wheeler was appointed Chairman of the Joint Chiefs of Staff by President Johnson. Vaught's assignment at the Pentagon changed with the appointment of Wheeler.

"I received a call telling me that General Wheeler was named Chairman and I was to report to the JCS staff," Vaught said. "I went down there, and nobody knew who I was. I told them General Wheeler had ordered me to report to the staff and that I would need a desk and classified file cabinet."

For the next two years, Vaught acted as a personal assistant, fact finder, and troubleshooter for the Chairman. U.S. involvement in Vietnam was expanding as U.S. advisers realized the South Vietnam government at the time did not possess the military or political capability to secure its territory. The Tonkin Gulf Incident would occur on August 4, 1964 providing the excuse for the Johnson administration to have American troops become more directly involved in the conflict. However, there were also hot spots in other parts of the world that required attention and military recommendations and/or response. It was in these types of situations that Wheeler used Vaught.

"I did whatever General Wheeler asked me to do," Vaught said. "My job was part diplomatic, part regular military, and part official representative. I spent time in the Middle East, Africa, and Latin America, often in civilian clothes."

One such example was the Dominican Republic Crisis in 1965. The Dominican Republic had been in a state of political instability since the assassination of long-time dictator Rafael Trujillo in 1961. Juan Bosch, founder of the anti-Trujillo Dominican

Revolutionary Party was elected President in December 1962 and inaugurated in February 1963. Bosch instituted leftist policies such as land distribution and nationalization of certain foreign holdings resulting in his overthrow in a military coup led by General Elias Wessin in late 1963. Wessin outlawed what he called Castroite Communist Doctrine. Power was turned over to a civilian triumvirate, but strikes and conflicts occupied much of the time until Spring 1965.

On April 28, 1965, the U.S. Ambassador to the Organization of American States, Ellsworth Bunker, sent a "Critic" priority message to Washington notifying the Johnson administration that the Dominican military had split into two factions with one faction arming civilians.

"Regret report situation deteriorating rapidly," stated the message. "Country team unanimously of the opinion that time has come to land the Marines...American lives are in danger."

Johnson conferred with his advisers and ordered 400 Marines to proceed to the Dominican capital at once. A briefing was scheduled for Congressional leaders that evening. At 11:30 a.m. the next morning, word was received by the Chairman's staff that General Wheeler was to testify at a 1:30 p.m. Senate hearing on the sequence of events that led to the crisis.

"That left us one and one-half hours to get the chronology together, but we made it," said Vaught.

Vaught had previously written a paper on the Dominican Republic, so he was familiar with the situation in the country.

On Day One, a USMC combat battalion was inserted by a combination of helicopters and LSTs to protect U.S. citizens, many of whom were located at the Ambassador Hotel in central Santo Domingo. Those who desired to leave were evacuated; however, fearing a "second Cuba" on the doorstep, Johnson quickly decided to raise the involvement of American forces to stabilize the situation and preserve a government that would be in line with American interests.

On the second night of the crisis, a battalion task force of the 82nd Airborne Division was flown into San Isidro Airfield. After two days of combat, the 82nd troops had taken the city away from rebel forces and returned it to friendly civilian control. Over the next few days, force levels increased with the addition of ground and naval units.

"We put a force of 32,000 on the ground in ten days along with a fleet of forty-one Navy ships to blockade the island," said Vaught. "We accomplished our combat mission with eight killed in action and less than forty wounded."

By April 30th, a cease-fire had been negotiated, and on May 5th, the Act of Santo Domingo was signed by representatives of the two Dominican military sides along with representatives of the Organization of American States. The Act provided for a general cease-fire, recognition of the International Security Zone, agreement to assist relief agencies, and the sanctity of diplomatic missions.

By mid-May, the decision was made to reduce the American military presence on the island and replace it with an Inter-American Peace Force (IAPF). Brazil agreed to provide a reinforced infantry battalion to the IAPF with Brazilian four-star General Hugo Alvim commanding the IAPF. By the end of May, the U.S. forces began to withdraw.

The 32,000 American troops initially committed to the conflict demonstrated the merits of deploying massive force rapidly rather than piecemeal deployment over a period of time.

"We were in and out in less than four months with everything turned over to the IAPF," said Vaught. "It was a good operation from our standpoint and demonstrated that we could work with our OAS partners to achieve goals in the hemisphere."

Argentina and Chile presented a problem of a different type for U.S. foreign and defense policy. The militaries of both countries wanted to control the eastern end of the Strait of Magellan, a navigable seaway between the southern tip of the South American continent mainland and the Tierra del Fuego archipelago. The strait is the one of the few natural navigable seaways between the Atlantic and Pacific Oceans and, while difficult to navigate, is considered easier to transit than the Drake Passage, which is a narrow passageway between the islands and Antarctica. A second dispute over the Beagle Channel, which separates the Grande Isle of Tierra del Fuego to the north from the smaller islands to the south, occurred when Argentina laid claim to several of the islands and the maritime jurisdiction around them.

By 1966, shipping was being affected by the ongoing dispute between the two countries. Wheeler sent Vaught to Chile to try and work out a solution with the military leaders to allow international shipping to continue to move through the two passages.

"It was my job to get the ships through," Vaught said. "Eventually, we worked out an agreement where Chile and Argentina would alternate control of the disputed areas on a monthly basis until a more formal arrangement could be worked out."

Vaught also acted as Wheeler's representative to South African military commanders on the subject of nuclear weapons. South Africa had already become an international outcast because of its continuing policy of discrimination against its majority Black population known as "Apartheid." The development of nuclear weapons would have only further isolated the South African government in the world community. Along with Rhodesia to its north, South Africa was intent on maintaining White minority control of the government with suppression of the Black majority in the country.

"There was concern in the Pentagon about what South Africa would do with nuclear weapons if it developed them," said Vaught. "The country's main conflict was with its own population; there were no outside nations really threatening it. The general staff in the country saw nuclear weapons as a means of maintaining minority control of the government and also as an ego thing. I finally convinced them that development of nuclear weapons would do South Africa more harm than good in the international community."

Vaught managed to get an informal agreement from the South African military leaders to delay development of nuclear weapons. The issue would again pop up in the 1970s after the issue of Apartheid became more controversial. As the White South African government tried to hold on against increasing unrest by its native Black majority population and widespread international boycotts and sanctions, it ultimately launched a nuclear weapons program in the late 1970s. Within a decade, South Africa developed six deliverable nuclear weapons, which it later dismantled as control of the government shifted to the Black majority in the mid-1990s.

On a personal level, the tour at the Pentagon provided the opportunity for two personal advancements. In November 1964, Vaught was promoted early to Lieutenant Colonel.

"I knew I wasn't in the zone for consideration because I did not have enough time in grade as a major," Vaught said. "One morning I was told I was out of uniform, and I was told to go check the list of newly promoted lieutenant colonels. I was surprised that I would be considered early, but I guess General Wheeler pulled some strings to get me promoted."

The time in the D.C. area also allowed Vaught to advance his education. He enrolled at George Washington University and earned a Master's in Government Administration in 1966.

"I knew if I was going to stay competitive for promotion that I needed to complete a master's degree," he said. "Government administration was an area of personal interest and a course of study that I knew would help me through the rest of my career."

Vaught was selected to attend the National War College with the class beginning in August 1966. Mid and senior level military officers who are most likely to be promoted to the most senior ranks in the military are chosen to attend the National War College in preparation for higher staff and command positions. Each class is composed of approximately 75% from land, sea, and air component officers with the remaining 25% drawn from Department of State employees and federal employees from other government agencies and departments. Classes concentrate on grand national strategy and the utilization of the various resources necessary to achieve that strategy.

Through nearly a year of classes, projects, distinguished lecturers, and the other activities students at the War College undertake, Vaught stood out from his peers. He was recognized as the student who asked the greatest number of in-depth, thought-provoking questions of the various lecturers.

Each student was required to complete a 3,500-word paper by the end of the class. At graduation, ten of the 140 papers submitted were chosen as best submissions. Vaught's paper was one of the ten chosen.

At the graduation ceremonies, Vaught was recognized by school commandant Admiral Fitzhue Lee, as the number one student in his class from the National War College. He was presented with a pair of gold cuff links by General Lyman Louis Lemnitzer on behalf of the students of the class.

Lieutenant Colonel Vaught ~1966

Chapter Seven

After graduating from the National War College, Vaught received orders to go to Vietnam for what would be his first of two tours in country. By this time in 1967, General William Westmoreland, Commander of the Military Assistance Command in Vietnam (MACV), was telling the Johnson administration and Pentagon officials back home that he was winning the war. Before looking specifically at Vaught's Vietnam service, a short overview of the history of Vietnam and how North and South Vietnam split into two countries will provide background for understanding American involvement in the Vietnam War, a defining event for the U.S. military of the 1960s, 1970s, and beyond.

Ho Chi Minh and his followers became communists essentially by accident. Generally, Ho and his lieutenants came from the historical mandarin class of Vietnamese aristocrats. The historical Vietnamese model followed that of China where the country was ruled by an emperor who governed through a hierarchy of mandarins, scholar administrators who gained their positions by demonstrating proficiency through a national examination process. The mandarins were initially a scholar bureaucracy who became a scholar aristocracy because poor farmers and peasants couldn't afford the cost of education for their sons to compete in the examinations.

After the French colonized Vietnam in the mid-1800s, many of the mandarins served the French colonial government in order to keep their place in society. A minority of the mandarins refused to serve the "European barbarians" and fell into disgrace and impoverishment. However, those who refused to serve the Europeans kept their place as leaders in the eyes of the peasants. It was from this group that Ho and his followers emerged as the leaders of the Vietnamese Communist Party.

Ho's father was dismissed from his bureaucratic post by the French for what was termed "nationalist activity." Ho made his way to France during World War I where he joined the French Socialist Party. He listened to debates closely when the French Socialists were deciding whether to remain with the tenets of the Second International of 1889 or join with the Third International organized by Vladimir Lenin in 1919. While Ho was not familiar with many of the political issues being debated because they were uniquely European in context, he came to the decision that the Third International (later called the Communist International or Comintern for short) sided more closely with the peoples of the colonial countries. Ho joined the radicals and became a founding member of the French Communist Party.

Ho attended the Paris Peace Conference where American President Woodrow Wilson and other Allied leaders were negotiating the Treaty of Versailles and the Covenant of the League of Nations. Believing in Wilson's famous Fourteen Points, Ho drew up a list of grievances of the Vietnamese against the French colonial regime. He petitioned the conference to allow Vietnam to establish an autonomous state within the French empire. No one from the American or other leading Allied delegations would agree to meet with Ho to hear his petition. From this experience, Ho determined that Wilson's policy of self-determination applied only to white Europeans, such as the Czechs and the Poles who had been under German and Austro-Hungarian domination, not to the yellow, brown, and black people of Asia and Africa who suffered under colonialism.

By 1924, Ho was sent to Canton, China by the Comintern where he was an interpreter with the political and military training mission attached to Dr. Sun Yat Sen's Kuomintang party, the party of China's recent national revolution. He formed the first secret communist organization in the history of Vietnam consisting of himself and eight other Vietnamese, most from his home province, in Canton. Ho traveled to Hangchow, Shanghai, and other Chinese cities talking up his new organization among other Vietnamese exiles. As word of Ho's teachings moved through the exile grapevine, the core of the revolutionary nationalist movement that was to lead North Vietnam after 1954 came together at this time as a proletarian political institution led by an indigenous aristocracy of Vietnamese. In addition to Ho, these included Truong Chinh, the senior theoretician; Le Duc Tho, who would negotiate with Henry Kissinger in Paris; Vo Nguyen Giap, the military leader who would become Vietnam's greatest general; and Pham Van Dong, who would become Prime Minister of North Vietnam. They were all descended from the scholar-gentry families of Vietnam who had refused to serve the French.

This core group returned to Vietnam with Ho in February 1941 after Japanese forces had occupied Vietnam and the rest of Indochina. The French colonial establishment was left in place by the Japanese because Vichy France collaborated with the Germans and Japanese during World War II. They returned to establish a national front organization, known under the Vietnamese nickname the Viet Minh, a broad alliance with non-communist Vietnamese organizations to "wage a war of national salvation and overthrow the Japanese, French and their Vietnamese jackals."

Ho and the Viet Minh had historical examples of Vietnamese resistance to foreign domination. It had taken the Vietnamese 1,000 years of revolt and sacrifice to win independence from China in A.D. 938. Over the next nearly 1,000 years until the French arrived in Indochina in the 1850s, every new dynasty that came to power in China invaded Vietnam only to be eventually driven out by the Vietnamese. These experiences had, through history, developed a central concept of military thought in Vietnam – a weaker force, properly handled, can defeat a stronger force by wearing it down through protracted warfare. The Vietnamese became experts in delaying actions, hit-and-run tactics, ambush and harassment by guerrilla units, and luring the stronger enemy to waste energy in the rain forests, mountains, and other difficult terrain features in Vietnam.

The military prowess and tradition of resistance to outside aggression was institutionalized in Vietnam by the time the French arrived. It was ingrained in the folklore of the country and the mentality of the peasants. Soldier-farmers were important as the Vietnamese conducted their "Southward Advance" from the Red River Delta to conquer Central Vietnam and the Mekong Delta. The Vietnamese peasant proved to be a formidable combatant. The French were able to initially overwhelm the country with superior organization and modern technology and weapons, but they could not break the will of the Vietnamese people.

During World War II, the Viet Minh essentially became a national movement claiming a half million followers by 1944, three-quarters of which were located in the north and central regions of the country. The Viet Minh had aided the Americans and their Allies during the war by providing help in rescuing downed air crews. When the Japanese took direct control of colonial administration in Indochina in Spring 1945, they confined themselves to the cities and coastal areas, leaving the interior of the country open to the Viet Minh who established governing authorities of "People's Committees" in the rural areas. Two days after the Japanese surrender was announced on August 15, 1945, the Viet Minh "Uprising Committee" unfurled a flag of revolution in Hanoi and called on the Vietnamese to revolt and "win back our ancestral land." By the end of August 1945, Ho and his party were the effective rulers of the north and the northern central provinces of Vietnam. Bao Dai, who succeeded as emperor of Vietnam on the death of his father in 1925 and ruled puppet governments under both the French and Japanese, abdicated to Ho when he handed over the dynastic seal and imperial sword to Viet Minh representatives in the imperial city of Hue in late August. On September 2, 1945, Ho read a Vietnamese declaration of independence and proclaimed the establishment of the Democratic Republic of Vietnam.

Anticipating a return of French colonial administration, Ho asked the United States government to establish a 25-year protectorate over Vietnam, similar to the protectorate the United States had established in the Philippines after the Spanish American War. He sent eleven letters and telegrams to U.S. Secretary of State James Byrnes over an 18-month period, but none were ever acknowledged. By the end of September 1946, the French army had returned to Vietnam and moved to discredit Ho's government. By the end of that year, Ho had concluded, "We apparently stand quite alone; we shall have to depend on ourselves."

On the American side, the Truman administration was worried about the possibility of the Soviet Union attempting to overrun the remainder of the European continent that it did not control at the end of World War II. Truman was eager to establish a defense alliance among the Allies of World War II and knew he needed French participation, air bases, and army installations to block any further possible advance by the Red Army in Europe. In order to cement this cooperation and the alliance, which would become NATO, the Truman administration agreed to the re-establishment of French colonial domination of Indochina.

In the sixteen months after Ho's declaration of independence, Giap and his associates in the military leadership had built an initial force of 5,000 guerrillas into a military force of 100,000. This force varied from guerrilla bands in the Mekong Delta to regular army battalions in Central and North Vietnam. Recruiting, training, and battle experience for the Vietnamese National Army continued uninterrupted until Giap exhausted the French forces in the mountains ringing the Red River Delta in a series of offensives from late 1949 to the fall of 1950. The French commander, General Marcel Carpentier ordered an emergency evacuation of the frontier towns around this area and suffered 6,000 casualties during a retreat along Colonial Route 4.

Over the next four years, Giap transitioned his army into a modern fighting force with the help of Chinese and Soviet heavy weapons until it put the final crushing defeat on the French colonial forces at Dien Bien Phu in May 1954, ending the First Indochinese War. Shortly after that battle, the French agreed to withdraw from their colonies under the 1954 Geneva Accords. The Accords established the 17th parallel as an arbitrary demarcation line for administration zones, but did not establish a formal partition of Vietnam into North and South. Ho's Democratic Republic of Vietnam was to administer the North while the South was administered by a French-supported State of Vietnam headed by Bao Dai, who had returned to the country in 1949 under French and U.S. sponsorship. Bao Dai's official title was Head of State, not emperor. The two zones were to be reunited through national elections in 1956.

The United States now chose to become directly involved in Vietnam. During the Battle of Dien Bien Phu, the French chief of staff had flown to Washington asking the Eisenhower administration to intervene directly in the war to help the French avoid defeat. Eisenhower's administration was divided, and he failed to get the congressional support needed to launch a large bombing campaign against the Viet Minh. However, in the Washington anti-communist atmosphere of the day spurred by Sen. Joe McCarthy and FBI Director J. Edgar Hoover's claims of communist infiltration in the government, the Eisenhower administration saw every nationalist uprising against colonialism as a communist plot orchestrated from Moscow.

The CIA maneuvered Bao Dai into giving the prime ministership of his government to Ngo Dinh Diem and also brought Edward Lansdale, ostensibly an Air Force officer, into Vietnam to forestall the spread of communism into the South. Lansdale operated with the OSS in World War II and moved to the Philippines after the war to help the Philippine government put down a communist uprising led by the Hukbalahap movement. Lansdale was successful in the Philippines and was sent to Vietnam to accomplish the same result. Lansdale was supposed to strengthen the position of Diem and build a nation in South Vietnam counter to the agreements of the Geneva Accords. The CIA, by this time, estimated that a national election, if held, would result in Ho Chi Minh gaining 80% of the popular vote throughout the country, resulting in the establishment of a "communist" government ruling all of Vietnam.

Lansdale operated out of the direct purview of the military always reporting to Washington through CIA channels. In October 1955, Lansdale helped Diem rig a plebiscite to depose Bao Dai as head of state and establish Diem as the President of the Republic of Vietnam. Lansdale helped Diem consolidate his position and that of his family and, almost singlehandedly, was responsible for establishing the country of South Vietnam with the appearance of a stable government. The direct result of Lansdale's achievement was to bring on the Second Indochinese War, or Vietnam War, as it was to become known in the United States.

However, Diem proved to be more interested in consolidating his influence in the cities, especially Saigon, and generally ignored the rural areas except to attempt to put down threats to his rule. One of the main methods used by the South Vietnamese troops to protect farmers in the South was to exile them to refugee camps far from the villages where they had ancestral and spiritual ties. Basically, all the South Vietnamese regime and American GIs accomplished was to antagonize the local peasantry.

The peasants in the rural areas, working with their water buffalo to eke out some kind of minimal existence for their families, basically saw the battle for control of the nation as one between a brutal, though generally popular regime in the North versus a brutal, and generally unpopular regime in the South. A disinterested observer seeing both the North and the South would have seen one telling difference between the two regimes. In North Vietnam, the government buildings and police stations were open to the public. In South Vietnam, these same structures were barricaded and entry was severely restricted. A government that has to guard itself from its own people can certainly not be considered the free, democratic state that South Vietnam was being sold as to the American people.

For the first four years after these events, Ho and his mandarins were consolidating their government in the North and dealing with a host of problems left over from the war with the French. This included brutally putting down a rebellion by

Catholic peasants in the North. However, Diem's regime was even more brutal in the South while attempting to drive Viet Minh influence out of the country. By 1963, the Viet Minh held influence over much of the South Vietnamese rural countryside while the Diem regime's control was centralized around Saigon and a few other cities. If the U.S. was to keep South Vietnam from falling to Ho and the Viet Minh, U.S. troops would have to become directly involved in the fighting, and Diem would have to go. The CIA maneuvered the assassination of Diem and his family just days before Kennedy was assassinated in Dallas, and by the next spring, the Johnson administration successfully got the Tonkin Gulf Resolution passed by Congress allowing LBJ to substantially expand the direct U.S. war effort. Lansdale retired in November 1963, and General William Westmoreland was appointed Commander of the Military Assistance Command Vietnam (MACV). Typical of the attitude with which the American military approached the war was Westmoreland's statement, "We're going to out-guerrilla the guerrilla and out-ambush the ambush... because we're smarter, we have greater mobility and fire-power, we have more endurance and more to fight for... And we've got more guts."

Vaught saw the early escalation of the American involvement in Vietnam from the perspective of his position on General Wheeler's JCS staff. When he was appointed MACV commander, Westmoreland announced a three-phase strategy for winning the war. Westmoreland's first phase called for slowing down the activity of the Viet Cong in South Vietnam. The second phase was to resume the offensive and destroy the enemy with search and destroy missions. The third and final phase was to restore South Vietnam as a unified country under the control of the Saigon government.

However, Westmoreland ran into trouble with his first phase since he wasn't slowing down the Viet Cong as quickly as he thought he was. Westmoreland consistently underestimated the ability of the enemy to replace losses. This led to calls for ever-increasing numbers of American troops in country. Westmoreland switched to his second phase of the strategy in 1966, just as Vaught was winding down with the JCS staff and preparing to go to the National War College.

Search and destroy missions involved having U.S. troops move out into the "boonies" to locate and destroy Viet Cong or North Vietnamese Army regular formations in the countryside. Search and destroy missions had many flaws that Westmoreland failed to acknowledge. They severely underestimated the enemy's abilities to match and exceed U.S. forces. Large numbers of Viet Cong troops would be killed or captured, but they were quickly replaced. Although enemy forces were pushed out of certain territories, as soon as the American forces left the North Vietnamese returned with more reinforcements. The missions also destroyed the countryside and rice paddies, weakening the economic productivity and creating inflation in South Vietnam. They created millions of refugees who lost their homes due to missions that called for setting fire to their bamboo houses. With many refugees and a damaged economic system, the missions hurt the political and social system in South Vietnam.

"Westy didn't know what was going on and wouldn't let anybody tell him," said Vaught.

As Vaught prepared to depart for duty in Vietnam in August 1967, he was following his old mentor General Creighton Abrams to the war zone. Abrams had been seriously considered for the position of Chief of Staff of the Army in 1964 before being appointed Vice Chief of Staff. Due to concerns about the conduct of the war in Vietnam, he was appointed Deputy Commander of MACV in May 1967 and would replace Westmoreland in command in June 1968.

Vietnam ~1967

Chapter Eight

When Vaught first arrived in Vietnam, he was assigned as the Deputy Commander 2nd Brigade, 1st Air Cavalry. Known as the Blackjack Brigade, it consisted of the 1st and 2nd Battalions, 5th Cavalry and 2nd Battalion, 12th Cavalry. The 2nd Brigade had been in Vietnam since 1965 when it went into the country as part of the first airmobile division in history. While the Brigade had been in country for over two years, there were no combat veterans who had been with the brigade that long. Combat tours during the Vietnam War consisted of a maximum of thirteen months. This led to an almost continuous replacement of individuals within each unit and a need for constant, ongoing training.

"I initially went out into the field to visit each unit to determine its state of training and how it conducted itself on missions," said Vaught. "When I arrived at each unit, I immediately told the commander 'I am not here to report on you, I am here to help you in any way I can. I'll just observe and make suggestions if I think things need to be improved.'"

One of the first things that stood out to Vaught was the action of troops returning from search missions in the field.

"They would get back into the base camp, drop their weapons, and hit the chow line," he said. "The most important thing a soldier can do when he returns from the field is clean his weapon and keep it close in case of a surprise attack. The enemy doesn't always work on your schedule, and you can be in big trouble with your guard down and a dirty weapon."

During much of 1967, units of the 1st Air Cavalry were involved in Operation Pershing in II Corps (the central region of South Vietnam). The operation was designed to disrupt and dismantle the Viet Cong infrastructure in the central region, which had been strong since the Viet Minh (the forerunner of the Viet Cong) had been fighting the French. A secondary mission in the operation was fighting against units of the regular 3rd Division of the North Vietnamese Army (NVA).

According to division after action reports, units of the 1st Air Cavalry pushed the Viet Cong infrastructure to the brink of collapse in the areas of Khanh Hoa, Phu Yen, and Binh Dinh between September 1967 and January 1968, the time Vaught was with the 2nd Brigade. The division's abundant use of helicopters gave it mobility and supply unheard of on the battlefield. The individual soldier needed to be equipped only with his weapon, ammunition, and water. Everything else was available from the air even to relatively inaccessible areas on the battlefield. Helicopters of all types were also routinely used for medical evacuation (medevac) of the wounded meaning they could quickly be transported from the battlefield to mobile surgical units for treatment.

"We located and devised a plan, which destroyed the 3rd North Vietnamese Army (NVA) Division headquarters on Bong San Mountain from which the 3rd NVA Division had been operating for five years," said Vaught.

By the end of 1967, the United States and its Army of the Republic of Vietnam (ARVN) and other allies seemed to be on the way to winning the war. They were getting much better on the battlefield and seemed to be disrupting and putting on the run both the Viet Cong and regular NVA units they came in contact with.

Westmoreland went on leave back to the United States and made such pronouncements in several speeches he gave. He believed that the allies had gained the upper hand and were steadily eroding the Viet Cong and NVA fighting strength and political underground in South Vietnam. Westmoreland led the administration and the American public to believe that major gains in the war could be expected in 1968 and that by the end of the year or sometime in 1969, American forces could be drawn down to only a token force to support a stable army and government in South Vietnam.

One thing that did bother Westmoreland was the situation in the two northernmost provinces in I Corps, the northern operating area of South Vietnam. In this area were concentrated most of the best of the NVA regular units as well as an extensive Viet Cong presence and important sections of the Ho Chi Minh Trail through which supplies for the NVA and Viet Cong traveled from North Vietnam through Laos and Cambodia to the I Corps area. As early as November 1967, Westmoreland decided to move the 1st Air Cavalry Division into I Corps to counter the enemy strength in the northern provinces. This move would significantly increase fire power against enemy units as well as block enemy infiltration through Laos and Cambodia and block enemy access to rice and other resources in South Vietnam that they needed to continue fighting.

Early in the war, Westmoreland had set up the Marine units in and around a large base camp at Khe Sanh. The concept was to maneuver NVA and Viet Cong units in the I Corps operating area into the vastly superior fire power of the Marines and destroy them. To some extent, this was the same concept the French had developed for Dien Bien Phu, but the Marines, frankly, were better than the French units had been. In December 1967, intelligence reports had picked up a large concentration of enemy forces along the Demilitarized Zone (DMZ) especially in the area of Khe Sanh. In early January 1968, Westmoreland ordered 1st Air Cav Commander Major General John Tolson to move his division's 1st and 3rd brigades into a series of firebases stretched along a 50 km section of Route 1 between Quang Tri City and Hue, the two most important cities in I Corps. Westmoreland anticipated this move would add support to the Marines as well as providing the flexibility to cripple Viet Cong sanctuaries in I Corps and cut the Ho Chi Minh Trail by Fall.

The 1st Air Cav began the move north on January 17, 1968. On the night of January 26th, the 5th Battalion, 7th Cavalry was spending the night at Quang Tri City airport when a salvo of sixty 122-mm rockets was fired at them. Lieutenant Colonel John Long, the battalion commander, was killed in the shelling, and Vaught was designated his replacement as CO of the 5th of the 7th.

"I got to the battalion at 2 p.m. the next day, and at 4 p.m. we were off on our first air assault," said Vaught, who was about to take a unit that he had never trained with into a major battle. "The 5th of the 7th was moved by helicopter to establish Landing Zone Jack 6 km southwest of the division HQ at Camp Evans and to act as a forward screen for the 1st Cavalry Headquarters encampment."

The move to command of the 5th of the 7th was to bring Vaught, in a couple of days, into the middle of what would become known as the Tet Offensive and some of the most intense fighting of the entire war.

"Tet was well underway, and no none knew exactly where the enemy was, or in what strength they were, or when the next attack would come," said Vaught. "It was important for any unit to give high consideration to local security arrangements."

The Tet Offensive began by accident on the night of January 29-30 when nine cities along the central coast of South Vietnam were attacked early. It began in earnest on the night of January 30-31 when the Viet Cong and NVA attacked 27 of South Vietnam's 44 provincial capitals, 5 of 6 autonomous cities, 58 of 245 district towns, and many smaller targets. General Giap thought this general offensive would lead to a popular uprising among the citizens of South Vietnam casting aside the government and paving the way for the establishment of a coalition government dominated by the Viet Cong. This government would then demand the withdrawal of all American and Allied troops and move toward reunification of the country under Ho Chi Minh's leadership.

The NVA had been attacking the base at Khe Sanh since January 20th and, by the beginning of the Tet Offensive, had 20,000 troops completely encircling the base of 6,000 Marines. However, as events moved forward, this appeared to be a feint to draw American troops away from Quang Tri City and Hue to the area of Khe Sanh.

The Tet Offensive provided the opportunity for the 1st Air Cav to demonstrate its air mobility and overall capabilities on the battlefield. For the only time in the history of armed conflict, a full division was deployed by air to areas among and behind enemy lines. It was no longer necessary to march up roads and be subject to ambush by enemy forces. The division units flew over the roads, getting between enemy units to cut roads, denying supplies and reinforcements from getting to embattled enemy units.

From February 1 to April 19, Lieutenant Colonel Vaught led the 5th Bn 7th Cav in the American response to the Tet Offensive in the North. Vaught and his battalion made the main effort in three major battles: the relief of Hue, the relief of Khe Sanh, and the movement in force into the A Shau Valley to cut the supply lines from North Vietnam into South Vietnam. The three battles were among the hardest fought engagements for American troops in the Vietnam War.

When Tet began in force, the enemy moved in strength into Quang Tri City and Hue. Threatened near Hue were the Military Assistance Command and the South Vietnamese Army compounds. Forces from the 3rd Brigade, 1st Air Cav moved immediately to seal off Hue from the north and west of the city. The 5th of the 7th and the 2nd of the 12th compromised this blocking force, which proved to be extremely valuable from a fire support standpoint. On February 5th, Vaught's battalion was airlifted to PK-17. This began a stretch of forty-two straight days in which Vaught's battalion would be surrounded by superior enemy forces while it fought through some extremely strong enemy positions to relieve Hue.

"We were directed to air assault two companies down there and move into the camp, which was still in friendly hands," Vaught said. "We did so, and brigade headquarters moved in there at the same time. We posted security around the perimeter and stayed there two days. Then I brought my other two companies down."

The two battalions took turns assaulting a strong enemy position just south of the village of Thon La Chu.

"We moved out of PK-17 in battalion formation as a reconnaissance in force and went through the countryside to the southwest of the camp, moving in the direction of Hue," Vaught said. "It was next to impossible to get any useful intelligence about where the enemy was or what their dispositions were."

"By the end of the first day, we began to encounter enemy outposts. Whether they were Viet Cong or NVA I don't know, but they clearly had rifles and had some kind of communications with mortars."

"Two days after we got out of there, we were moving across a field toward woods where the 2nd of the 12th had been engaged in heavy fighting about five days before. We decided to do a little probing to see what we were up against."

"We moved out attacking and got into a very heavy firefight at the edge of the woods. Mortars and machine guns were coming at us. We got to the edge of the village, but I realized I was taking three to four casualties per minute and I couldn't see that we were achieving very much."

"I called the brigade commander and told him I was going to pull my battalion back to woods just to the west of where we were and reconsider how to conduct a more effective attack."

"Based upon what we learned from our two front companies, we found out there were reinforced concrete bunkers surrounded by concertina/barbed wire. We were going to have to reduce a fortified position if we went back in there."

Vaught moved his battalion to the center of the woods and dug in. For the next several days, the battalion tried to determine what size force it was encountering and gained additional training for a new assault. Using binoculars from a building at the edge of the woods, Vaught saw a flag flying over a building that was obviously serving as a headquarters.

"There they were, flying a flag over the building, certain they were in control of everything around," Vaught said. "We were about 2,000 meters from them, my one battalion against what could be deduced as a large force with the headquarters in the building."

The actual size of the enemy force would not be known until after the battle. A combination of mortars, aerial rocket artillery, and naval gunfire were used against enemy positions every day.

Vaught took time before another assault on the position to instruct the battalion on the proper use of demolitions, satchel and pole-mounted ten-pound charges, against bunkers and hedgerows.

"I knew we probably weren't well trained on attacking fortified positions," Vaught said. "I reflected on training I had much earlier in the Army and my experiences in Korea and elsewhere. My S-3, Major Charlie Baker, put together a little training area in our position, and we ran every rifle squad in the battalion through attacking a fortified position including how to use Bangalore torpedoes and satchel charges and how to cut the wire and designate a man to go in. We even trained about eight flame thrower teams in case we needed them."

During this time, division commander, Major General John Tolson moved two additional battalions into the area for a final assault on Thon La Chu on February 21st. Vaught's men pushed into the fiercely defended tree line near the northwest corner of the village. Vaught maneuvered troops with M72 antitank rocket launchers onto berms to fire ahead of his advancing troops, keeping the enemy pinned down in the bunkers. Light H13 observation helicopters ranged overhead hitting the backside of the bunkers with machine gun fire. Ground point men used radios and smoke grenades so that when the order to cease supporting fire came, men rushed forward to push pole charges and satchel charges into bunker openings caving in the bunkers. These tactics resulted from the training Vaught had given the battalion prior to the final assault.

"I attacked with two companies abreast in columns that went into the fortified area," said Vaught. "In about an hour and a half, we had reduced fifteen positions. We got through the concertina wire, and the soldiers were putting satchel charges right on the bunkers and blowing them out. We continued to attack throughout the day, opened up the woods, and by the end of the day we had conquered it."

A captured enemy soldier from Thon La Chu provided information about the force Vaught's battalion had pushed out of the city. The soldier said 1,000 NVA troops had been in the bunkers, rarely leaving them. They were supplied by Viet Cong who brought food, water, and ammunition. This was the enemy force that had proved difficult to overcome until the final assault. Chasing the enemy forces from Thon La Chu is considered the turning point in the Battle of Hue.

The Air Cav battalions kept pressure on the North Vietnamese as they pursued them through hedgerows and palm trees. They pushed through enemy supply and staging areas as they made the final drive into Hue. On the morning of February 22nd, Bravo Company from the 5th of the 7th air assaulted into Hue to join up with armored personnel carriers of the 3rd Squadron, 5th Armored Cavalry.

The rest of Vaught's battalion came under heavy enemy fire approximately one kilometer from Hue at the An Hoa Bridge. He called in heavy fire support throughout the day before breaking off the battle for the night. On the morning of February 23rd, Vaught resumed the push toward Hue with the help of six M-48 tanks and some armored personnel carriers that had been attached to his battalion.

"We took the tanks and made a tank-infantry team that went along the wall on the road that goes just west of the wall on the outskirts of Hue," Vaught said. "I took another company with some tanks through the woods, around to the right and ended up cutting across QL 1 about halfway between where we had been held up and Hue. At the same time, my S-3 took a company along the wall to the bridge. I turned our company around and attacked the fortified position from the rear, reducing it quickly."

The next day, the 5th of the 7th reached the southwestern corner of the Citadel in Hue, and the Battle of Hue was considered over. Clean-up actions took place on the 25th. With the battle for Hue over, the battalion returned to Camp Evans.

"Once you make contact with the enemy, you pursue him relentlessly," said Vaught. "A determined enemy with good firepower can stop you on the battlefield. Maintaining your momentum and immediately bringing to bear firepower and intel are your best course of action to defeat the enemy."

"We left with a full battalion, over 600 men," said Vaught. "We went forty-two days with the battalion in operational circumstance where we had to fight, shoot every day as best as I recall. When we got back to Camp Evans, we had 312 men. Maybe half the people who left us during the fight, wounded one way or another and gone out through MEDEVAC channels, came back to the battalion. That allowed me to rebuild the battalion very quickly."

The Battle of Hue effectively ended the Tet Offensive operations. It was the longest and hardest fought of all the engagements. That it was a defeat for the NVA and the Viet Cong was also noteworthy. The Tet Offensive resulted in a massive military defeat for the North Vietnamese. The Viet Cong were so decimated during the various battles that they effectively ceased to be a military force for the remainder of the war. Estimates credited the 1st Air Cavalry Division alone with killing more than 3,200 NVA and Viet Cong soldiers while clearing critical territory, recapturing towns and cities, and securing a vital stretch of Route 1, Vietnam's most valuable land supply route.

The 3rd Brigade, which included the 5th of the 7th, was credited with winning a month-long battle for critical northern and western approaches to Hue while defeating large enemy forces from parts of nineteen battalions, cutting enemy supply and reinforcement lines and insuring the encirclement of the larger battlefield. The expectations of an uprising by the civilian population of South Vietnam, in support of the North Vietnamese attack, were grossly mistaken. The NVA was in such a depleted state that strong pursuit of its retreating units could have resulted in the battle that ended the war.

"After Tet, General Abrams wanted to pursue the NVA over the border into North Vietnam," said Vaught. "If we had been allowed to pursue that strategy, the war would have been over in short order."

Despite the massive defeat for the North Vietnamese forces on the battlefield, the Tet Offensive paved the way to eventual victory by North Vietnam and reunification of the country seven years later. In the initial stages of the offensive, the NVA and Viet Cong had gotten into all the major cities and most of the provincial capitals, including Saigon where the enemy had successfully entered the American Embassy compound. Newsreels sent back to the United States of these apparent North Vietnamese successes went a long way toward turning a majority of the American citizens against the war. Americans had been hearing from Westmoreland, during his speech tour in late 1967, and from the Johnson administration how American forces had turned the tide against the North and that victory in Vietnam would soon be in hand. The pictures sent back home by the media during the Tet Offensive contradicted these claims. The Tet Offensive was a military defeat for North Vietnam, which turned into a propaganda victory, paving the way for increased opposition to the war back home in the United States as the American public became increasingly tired of the prolonged conflict.

"Americans don't like long wars, and a majority of American citizens do not like the military because their ancestors came to this country to get away from conflicts in Europe and other parts of the world," Vaught said. "By the end of Tet, the Vietnam War had already gone on longer than World War II, and Americans were tired of it regardless of what was happening on the battlefield."

After the Battle of Hue, the 1st Air Cav consolidated its gains in the area west of Hue and Quang Tri City and kept the enemy retreating from population centers. The Air Mobile battalions moved through the dense jungles in the area capturing large quantities of enemy weapons, food, and ammunition in secret enemy sanctuaries. The division also moved into the northern coastal plain to deny the enemy rice crops and recruits and to further destroy the Viet Cong infrastructure.

At the end of March, the 1st Air Cav command turned its attention to Operation Pegasus and the relief of the Khe Sanh combat base. This operation, which began April 1st, involved a combination of Marine units and the 1st Air Cav along with the South Vietnamese 3rd Airborne Task Force. The Marines would attack west along Route 9 toward Khe Sanh while the 1st Air Cav units would leapfrog along the high ground on both sides of Route 9 and move constantly west toward Khe Sanh.

"The operational responsibility was given to the commanding general of the 1st Air Cavalry, General Tolson, and he came up with the plan," Vaught said.

The 5/7th was involved in the first day landings when the 1st Air Cav, using its air mobility capability to perfection, put three battalions of troops within 5 miles of the Khe

Sanh combat base. Vaught's battalion was airlifted to Landing Zone Cates to the northeast of the Khe Sanh combat base.

"We went in there about two o'clock in the afternoon," said Vaught. "It was an area that no one knew whether there was enemy or not, but in Vietnam, especially in those days, you always had to assume the enemy might be there. We fired a few suppressive rounds and then made the air assault and got to the ground."

The next day, the battalion moved out on reconnaissance and got into major contact with a large NVA force. Vaught's troops overran a mortar position and cleared the area before setting up an operating base. The weather was perfect for airmobile operations, and the speed and mobility of the 1st Air Cav units, combined with the exceptional fire support that both ground-based and air mobile artillery provided, caused the enemy units to ultimately drop their weapons and flee in the face of the determined American advance. Two companies were sent down a ridge line to the west of Khe Sanh behind the enemy positions conducting the siege on the Marine base.

"I got permission to fly into Khe Sanh to coordinate with the local Marine commander," Vaught said. "As we landed the helicopter, somebody started mortaring the place. I jumped out of the chopper with the staff I had along and ran into a bunker. The helicopter took off to get some fuel and flew around until I called him to come back and pick me up."

Vaught told the Marine executive officer (the regimental commander was not in the bunker) that within the next two days, the 5th of the 7th was going to conduct an assault up to the fence line. The Marine exec told Vaught there was a lot of enemy out there. Vaught responded that flying over it didn't seem that way, but it didn't make any difference because he had been ordered to assault when ready.

"What I'm asking you to do is open your fence and allow us to bring wounded into your bunkers if we have a lot of casualties out there and also to coordinate fire support with anything you may have available to help us," Vaught said.

The next day, the attack began after considerable artillery bombardment of the area.

"I put the whole battalion parallel to the fence along the edge of Khe Sanh," Vaught said. "There were about eighty NVA hiding in the trenches and bunkers. They were in terrible condition from the bombing the B-52s had been doing prior to our movement. It was clear somebody had decided to pull most of them out, or they had simply left during the bombing. We cleared the enemy from the northern part of Khe Sanh and set up a battalion defensive position."

At the same time, the 2nd of the 7th battalion was coming up from the south and had run into determined opposition. For some reason, the attack of the two battalions didn't get coordinated, and Vaught's battalion never got an order to attack from the rear of the NVA opposing the 2nd of the 7th. Nevertheless, the 5th of the 7th was one of the units that officially relieved Khe Sanh on April 8th. After some mop-up operations, the relief officially ended on April 15th.

Now attention for the 1st Air Cav shifted to Operation Delaware and the A Shau Valley, a remote area near the Laotian border, through which much of the NVA supplies traveled from North Vietnam to its units operating in the South. After five days of bombing by B-52s against anti-aircraft positions noted on initial reconnaissance, the 5th of the 7th was among the first units in the air assault into the A Shau Valley. When the proposed landing areas proved to be too small, Vaught assigned men with Ranger training to rappel down ropes with chain saws, from the helicopters, to cut trees and expand the landing areas. On the second day of the operation, Vaught's battalion moved southwest to block Route 548, which entered the valley from Laos to the west. B Company was placed on high ground and C Company on low ground, while A Company went out to the west toward the enemy command post.

"We were engaged pretty heavily right from the start," Vaught said. "Obviously, that was a very high priority road from the NVA's standpoint. Right before dark, we set ambush team at each opening into our area. Just after dark, we ate chow, then moved 1 km and dug in. That night, the enemy attacked our command post and wound up being ambushed by our troops."

The next day, Captain Mike Davison, C Company commander, asked Vaught to take a look at his position, which was set up to interdict enemy tanks that were reported to be in the area. Vaught and his driver strapped six 5-gallon cans of water onto a truck and drove out to C Company about one kilometer away.

"He had done a good job of putting them in, and I was satisfied with what they had," Vaught said. "He had the company well disposed across the armor approach."

On the way back to the command post that evening, some NVA started firing at the truck.

"The NVA were trying to withdraw and harass us at the same time," Vaught said. "Some rounds were flying by us and the driver gunned the truck, which was not in very good shape. The road was about a 10% grade coming down from where C Company was located, and the damn thing lost its brakes."

The driver tried to gear down the truck and was bumping it into the side of the bank next to the road to try and slow it down. Vaught jumped out of the vehicle and tried to slow it down by grabbing the truck platform. As the truck struck a rut and rolled over, Vaught suffered a broken back and the sergeant driving suffered a compound fracture of the leg and was pinned under the steering wheel.

"We lay like that for about thirty minutes until the battalion surgeon, Dr. Jeffrey Kahlen, and his medical team supervised getting the truck off of me," Vaught said. "Later that evening, Major Fitch, my company commander and pilot, with guidance from my Black Hats, flew 22 miles in total darkness to our A Shau battalion command post and medevacked me and four other wounded soldiers back to Camp Evans."

For his attempts to stop the truck and save the driver, Vaught was awarded the Soldier's Medal under General Order Number 6394. The order stated in part: "Lieutenant Colonel Vaught distinguished himself by heroism on 19 April 1968, while serving as commanding officer of the Headquarters and Headquarters Company, 5th Battalion, 7th Cavalry. When the vehicle in which he was riding lost its brakes and was out of control on a mountain road, Lieutenant Colonel Vaught, disregarding his own safety, jumped off the vehicle and grasped the platform in an attempt to slow it down. The vehicle hit a rut and flipped over throwing the driver to the ground. At this time, Lieutenant Colonel Vaught tried to stop the vehicle from falling on the driver. The driver was able to roll to safety, but the vehicle fell on Lieutenant Colonel Vaught seriously wounding him. His concern for the welfare of his fellow soldiers and devotion to duty are in keeping with the highest traditions of the military service and reflect great credit upon himself, his unit, and the United States Army."

Vaught's first tour in Vietnam was over as he would spend the next five months recovering from his injuries for which he received the Purple Heart. The first month was at the big hospital in Camp Drake in Tokyo, Japan. Then he was moved to Walter Reed Medical Center in Washington, D.C., which was fortunate because it allowed him to continue his career.

Reflecting back on his first tour in Vietnam, Vaught said there didn't appear to be a national strategy with regard to Vietnam.

"Having been a student at the National War College and a member of the staff at the Joint Army Staff and Joint Chiefs of Staff, it was clear to me that our strategy was ill-defined," Vaught said. "No one knew what our national strategy was with regard to Vietnam, and they did not know what our theater operational concept was for winning the war or conducting campaigns that would lead to some clearly identifiable achievement."

Vaught said the only thing he could determine was that the Army was conducting a lot of tactical exercises, experimenting to find out better ways of "charging around the jungle fighting and living to fight another day."

"As for unit-level actions, I thought the units conducted themselves very well for the most part," Vaught said. "We could take terrain, we could take hills, we could kick the enemy out. In my first term in Vietnam it was very frustrating because we conquered areas that had already been held once, given up, and taken back again."

Vaught said his main criticism was that the Army never got its act together very well when it came to knowing what it was there to do.

"I believe that after Tet, we had the war won and just let it slip away," Vaught said. "The enemy had shot their wad trying to conquer us and it was all over. If, at that time, we could have pressed on and followed the enemy to the north and maybe gone to Hanoi, but we just let the opportunity fade away."

"I was just a lowly battalion commander, but having been to the National War College I was supposed to think about strategy and things like that. I couldn't help but wonder – What in the hell is going on, and where does all this lead to?"

Vietnam ~1968

Chapter Nine

Vaught spent a total of five months, mostly at Walter Reed Medical Center, recovering from the broken back and other injuries suffered in the truck accident in the A Shau Valley. He also had to fight the most important fight of his career to this point.

"When it was coming time for me to be released from Walter Reed, the doctors there recommended I appear before a medical board with the intent of giving me a medical discharge with 100% disability pay," said Vaught. "However, I didn't want to get out of the Army. I was eligible for retirement, but I felt my career was still rising and there were more challenges ahead if I stayed in. I felt I was on my way to flag rank."

Vaught contacted an Army doctor he had been stationed with previously who was now high up in the chain of command. The doctor agreed to help him stop the attempt at a medical discharge and stay in the Army.

"I was fully healed, and there was no reason to give me a medical discharge," said Vaught. "After reviewing my medical records, the doctor I knew agreed with me, and I was able to return to active duty."

After he had recovered physically, but while the question about whether he would remain on active duty was being decided, Vaught was assigned to the Office of the Secretary of Defense, Public Affairs Division. His initial assignment was to act as a liaison to veterans' organizations, meeting with members of groups such as the American Legion and Veterans of Foreign Wars.

"I would meet the groups at the front of the Pentagon as they arrived and take them to the Public Affairs office for a briefing and, finally, to meet with the Secretary of Defense Clark Clifford for a short time," Vaught said. "There was a lot of opposition to the Vietnam War in the country, especially from student groups, beginning in 1968. The veterans' organizations were strongly on the military's side and opposed to the demonstrations."

Vaught met with many different groups of visitors to the Pentagon during his time in Public Affairs. However, to a combat veteran of two wars and an officer who had been in on some of the critical Army decisions while serving General Wheeler at the Pentagon, it wasn't the type of assignment that appealed to him.

"My philosophy, when given a job, was to do it to the best of my ability regardless of what it was, but Public Affairs wasn't really the type of job I wanted in the Army," Vaught said.

Fortunately, after serving for five months in the Public Affairs Division, Vaught was promoted to colonel.

"There were no jobs in Public Affairs for colonels, so I was transferred to the Office of the Secretary of Defense for International Security Affairs," Vaught said. (That is OSD-ISA in Pentagon parlance.)

He was assigned to the Latin America area, which included all of Central and South America, where he shared an office with Colonel Brent Scowcroft of the Air Force. Scowcroft was a fast-track Air Force officer who would go on to become Military Assistant to President Nixon in 1972 and was named Deputy Assistant to the President for National Security Affairs in August 1973, a post formerly held by General Alexander

Haig who was now acting as the President's Chief of Staff. Scowcroft retired from the Air Force in December 1975 as a Lieutenant General. After his retirement, Scowcroft went on to become National Security Advisor to President Gerald Ford and later held the same position with President George H.W. Bush.

The mission of ISA was to keep up with world events, especially as they affected countries within the U.S. sphere of influence. ISA leaders prepared briefings and papers about what was going on in the world, projected what may happen in the near future, and prepared suggestions to the Secretary of Defense regarding what to do about these events, if anything. In addition, it was part of a State Department chaired planning group for foreign assistance planning.

"About 50% of my time was spent on the ground in various hot spots in Central and South America," Vaught said. "When I was in Washington, I was the OSD representative to the U.S. State Department Intergovernmental Planning Group. The State Department runs foreign assistance programs, and this group was part of that effort. It made policy and funding recommendations to the Secretary of State who is in charge of Military Assistance Programs for the President."

By the time Vaught arrived at ISA, there was a new administration in town as Richard Nixon had succeeded Lyndon Johnson in January 1969 as President of the United States. Upon Nixon's assumption of office, Henry Kissinger assumed the position of Nixon's National Security Advisor. As Henry Kissinger was considered an expert on European affairs and well versed on Asian affairs, Latin America had been outside the scope of his real expertise.

Scowcroft had recently written a paper on providing measured assistance to Colombia because ISA was trying to get something moving in Colombia to help the government. Since the early 1960s, the Colombian government had been engaged in armed conflict against both left-wing insurgents and right-wing paramilitary organizations. Scowcroft's paper came to Kissinger's desk where he read it and was impressed.

"The phone in our office rang, and Kissinger was on the other end of it," said Vaught. "From that time on, Scowcroft worked for Kissinger, and I was left with the rest of the countries in Central and South America."

At least since the Spanish-American War, the countries of Central and South America, as well as the islands of the Caribbean, had essentially been treated as colonies by the government of the United States. Virtually without exception, the governments of those countries were oligarchies where a small group of wealthy land and business owners, including the Catholic Church, controlled all the power and most of the population was comprised of peasants struggling to eat and live. Additionally, American corporations had made significant inroads into many of those countries owning and controlling much of the best land and other natural resources, paying extremely low wages and taking the profits back north to the United States.

Two examples of heavy-handed U.S. government actions provide a glimpse of how the United States treated Latin America. In 1878, the French had started to build a canal across the Isthmus of Panama, which was then a part of Colombia. The canal would significantly cut the time at sea for cargo ships sailing from Europe and the eastern United States to ports on the west side of South America and the Orient. The New Panama Canal Company, a French company, held the rights to the canal project but had been unable to complete it due to tropical diseases and engineering problems.

When President Theodore Roosevelt assumed office, the completion of the canal took on new significance for the U.S. government. A believer in the sea power strategy of Captain Alfred Thayer Mahan, USN, that the nation who controlled the seas would control the globe, Roosevelt immediately began to build up the U.S. Navy.

The completion of the Panama Canal also took on utmost significance for Roosevelt. He agreed to have the U.S. government pay $40 million for the rights to build the canal and began negotiations with the government of Colombia for a 50-mile strip of land, later known as the Panama Canal Zone, across the isthmus. Roosevelt offered $10 million for the rights to the land, but the government of Colombia refused. So, Roosevelt arranged a revolution led by the chief engineer of the New Panama Canal Company. When the revolt began in Panama, Roosevelt immediately sent the battleship *Nashville* to the area and debarked a detachment of Marines to support the new government of the now Republic of Panama. The canal was built and remained under the control of the United States until 1977 when the Carter-Torrijos Treaties provided for transition of control of the canal to the Panamanian government by 1999.

Another example of the United States and its citizens doing what they wanted in Latin America is provided by the case of Samuel Zemurray. Having operated as a young businessman in New Orleans, Zemurray went to Honduras in 1910 where he bought 5,000 acres of land on the Cuyamel River and founded the Cuyamel Fruit Company. After purchasing more land, Zemurray found himself deeply in debt and paying high taxes to the Honduran government. He appealed to U.S. Secretary of State Philander Knox who declined help.

Zemurray returned to New Orleans where he met with deposed Honduran president Manuel Bonilla. They planned a revolution to put Bonilla back into power. Zemurray smuggled Bonilla back into Honduras where he launched a revolution against the government of President Davila with the help of American mercenaries. Without going into detail, Bonilla came back into power with the support of the American government. After returning to power, Bonilla granted land concessions and low taxes to Zemurray, which saved the Cuyamel Fruit Company.

Zemurray ultimately sold the Cuyamel Fruit Company to the United Fruit Company in 1930 and retired from the banana business. By 1933, United Fruit was suffering from the Great Depression having seen the value of its stock plunge by ninety percent prompting Zemurray to return to the business by acquiring the depressed stock, voting out the sitting board of directors, and reorganizing the company.

United Fruit was already operating in other Latin American countries including Guatemala. In 1901, the government of Guatemala hired the United Fruit Company to manage the country's postal service, and in 1913, the United Fruit Company created the Tropical Radio and Telegraph Company. By 1930, United Fruit had absorbed more than twenty rival firms, acquiring a capital of $215,000,000 making it the largest employer in Central America. By 1954, United Fruit was heavily invested in Guatemala with control over the country's best land and ports on the Atlantic Ocean. It was said that the government of Guatemala's wishes were often subservient to those of United Fruit.

In 1944, the government of Guatemala was overthrown in the October Revolution, and Juan José Arévalo-Bermejo was elected president. Arévalo signed a labor protection law in 1947 that specifically targeted United Fruit.

In 1950, Jacobo Árbenz-Guzman succeeded Arévalo as president. Árbenz advocated social and political reforms including unionization and land reform. In 1952,

Árbenz pushed through the Agrarian Reform Act to remedy the unequal land distribution among the populace. Árbenz was already being accused of being under Communist influence by the land-owning upper class in Guatemala and a portion of the military. In March 1953, uncultivated lands owned by the UFC were to be expropriated with a proposed compensation plan. In October 1953 and in February 1954, the Guatemalan government took another 150,000 acres of uncultivated land from the United Fruit Company, bringing the total amount of appropriations to almost 400,000 acres. The Guatemalan government proposed to pay United Fruit a total of $1.7 million based on the company's declared value and taxes paid.

However, for years United Fruit had been undervaluing the land to keep the taxes low. After the land expropriation began, United Fruit began lobbying the U.S. government in an attempt to draw them into their confrontation with Árbenz. In April 1954, the U.S. State Department delivered a note to the Árbenz government demanding that Guatemala pay $15,854,849 for just the United Fruit properties expropriated on the Pacific Coast. The Guatemalan government refused.

As early as December 1953, the CIA had been recruiting pilots and training rebel fighters for the purpose of overthrowing the Árbenz government. On May 24th, the U.S. Navy established a sea blockade on Guatemala, and on June 18th, rebel forces led by Castillo Armas and supported by the CIA crossed the border into Guatemala. Despite initial reversals, the revolution was successful with Árbenz resigning as president on June 27th. Once again, United Fruit had been successful in removing a foreign government it considered harmful to its business interests.

These examples demonstrate the U.S. government's tendency to work in the interests of its own goals or the needs and goals of its corporations, often counter to the desires of the government and desires of the general population in Latin American countries. By the mid-1950s, there was considerable distrust of U.S. motives and interests in the region.

On January 1, 1959, Fidel Castro was successful in his revolution to overthrow U.S.-backed Cuban dictator Fulgencio Batista. Initially, the governments of both the United States and U.S.S.R. supported the new Castro government. But, charges of Castro being a Communist made by Cuban émigrés who had fled to Miami, Florida during the revolution and the tendency of the Eisenhower administration to believe these charges led to a CIA plan to attempt to overthrow Castro with the ill-fated Bay of Pigs invasion of April 1961. After the Bay of Pigs, Castro became solidly in the Soviet camp resulting in a hostile Communist government ninety miles south of Florida.

Castro's number two man, Che Guevara, a true socialist revolutionary, warned that the Cuban revolution endangered all American possessions in Latin America. Guevara was the Cuban government official involved in the attempt to bring Soviet offensive nuclear missiles into Cuba, which resulted in the Cuban Missile Crisis of October 1962. After that was unsuccessful, Che spent the remaining five years of his life attempting to "export the revolution" to other countries. He was ultimately captured and executed in Bolivia by the Bolivian military aided by information from the CIA.

It was in this atmosphere of Latin American distrust of U.S. government motives and U.S.S.R. attempts to foment revolutions in Latin American countries that Vaught worked in the ISA.

In general, Vaught said the Catholic Church was more influential in Latin America than either the United States or the U.S.S.R. was.

"The Catholic Church runs much of that part of the world," Vaught said. "It holds title to a lot of the land while much of the general population is reduced to sharecropping. The key to success in improving Latin America is looking for ways to get the church to become more forthcoming in programs to help the populace."

Working with the U.S. ambassadors and military attachés in each country, Vaught established a two-way system of communication.

"Each attaché would keep me informed, and I would do the same with them when policy questions came up and decisions were being made," Vaught said.

One incident of a Soviet-backed coup attempt took place in Chile in early 1970 when rebel forces attempted to overthrow President Eduardo Frei-Montalvo.

"The CIA got information that a coup against Frei was being planned," Vaught said. "The CIA's Chief of Station and the attaché hopped a plane to the Pentagon."

According to information developed by the CIA, 5,000 hardcore communists from Russia and Eastern Europe were going to take over the Chilean capital and run the country. Working through the night, plans were made to remove President Frei from the capital, isolate the rebels in the capital, and defeat the coup.

"The geography of Chile makes this possible," said Vaught. "While it is nearly 4,000 miles long, Chile is less than 100 miles wide in most places. This means that nearly eighty percent of the country is generally isolated from the capital of Santiago."

The geography worked for both sides. If the coup was successful in eliminating President Frei and taking over the capital, it would be difficult to dislodge the rebels. By the same token, removing Frei and other government officials from Santiago made it easy to isolate the rebels while the government remained in power.

"After our people got back to Chile, they were successful in getting President Frei to leave the capital before the coup was launched," said Vaught. "When the rebels landed in Santiago, the Presidential Guard and other units of the Chilean army cut off access to Santiago and the president declared martial law and the necessary steps were taken to inform the Chilean population what was happening and the situation was under control. After about five days, the rebels left with very few casualties on either side. It became known in the Pentagon as 'the coup that wasn't a coup.'"

After eighteen months in the ISA, Vaught received orders back to Vietnam, this time as a Liaison Officer to the South Vietnamese military from the U.S. Army Combat Development Command in Vietnam.

Vaught receiving the Legion of Merit during his promotion to Colonel in 1970

Chapter Ten

The Vietnam War Vaught returned to in the Fall of 1970 was considerably changed from the one he left nearly three years earlier. Richard Nixon had been elected president in November 1968 partly due to his "secret" plan to end the war and his "peace with honor" pledge to the American voters. No such plan actually existed; it was all campaign rhetoric. Nixon wasn't nicknamed "Tricky Dick" for nothing.

After the Tet Offensive of 1968, a majority of American public opinion had turned against the war. The fact that Tet was a major military victory for the United States and its South Vietnamese allies, even though it proved to be a psychological and political defeat among American citizens, gave Nixon some wiggle room as he took office in January 1969.

In July 1969, Nixon announced the "Nixon Doctrine" and the first of what would become many American troop withdrawals from South Vietnam until the last American troops were finally withdrawn in March 1973. The doctrine said the United States would assist in the defense and development of allies and friends but would not undertake all the defense of the free nations of the world. With the announcement of the Nixon Doctrine and the beginning of troop withdrawals, Nixon began the process of "Vietnamization" of the war – the gradual turning over of the war effort to South Vietnamese fighting units.

Vietnamization was in full swing by the time Vaught returned to Vietnam. He was assigned as a Senior Military Advisor in the Combat Development Command whose mission was to coordinate combat development projects in South Vietnam and to facilitate new ideas and urgent requirements of the Army of the Republic of Vietnam (ARVN). Initially, Vaught went into the field to talk to troops and their commanders up to and including the division level. In addition, he went to areas where operations were being conducted to observe tactics and techniques that were being used and report his observations.

One of the major operations Vaught went to observe was Lam Son 719, an operation to interdict the flow of supplies from North Vietnam down the Ho Chi Minh Trail to North Vietnamese Army (NVA) units in South Vietnam. He visited 24th Corps headquarters and ARVN HQ where planning for the operation was being conducted.

"Conceptually the plan seemed sound, but they didn't wargame the plan before the attack was launched due to security reasons," Vaught said. "The Vietnamese commanders did not know the total concept of operations, so in execution the plan was sort of doomed from the start."

In 1970, American and South Vietnamese forces had launched a total of thirteen major operations into eastern Cambodia to destroy the base areas and the approximately 40,000 North Vietnamese and Viet Cong troops in eastern Cambodia border regions. Cambodia was officially a neutral country with a weak military ruled by pro-communist Prince Norodom Sihanouk. While Sihanouk was out of the country in March 1970, pro-US general Lon Nol launched a coup, deposed the absent Sihanouk, and received emergency powers from the Cambodian National Assembly. The United States immediately recognized Lon Nol government.

Shortly after Lon Nol seized power, South Vietnamese and American forces began their attacks on North Vietnamese bases that Sihanouk had allowed to be established in Cambodia's eastern border regions. These operations became known as the Cambodian

Incursion. Having received advance knowledge of the planned attacks from spies in South Vietnam, NVA troops and headquarters remained elusive during these operations, many retreating westward as the attacks began, resulting in far fewer than hoped for casualties. However, U.S. and ARVN troops were successful in destroying a number of bases and capturing or destroying large quantities of supplies. The destruction of these supplies essentially eliminated any opportunity for the NVA to conduct major military operations in South Vietnam during the remainder of 1970, making the Cambodian Incursion a success for the Allies.

Again, however, success on the battlefield didn't lead to success on the U.S. home front. The American public deemed the incursion into Cambodia an escalation of the Vietnam War. Demonstrations against the war and this perceived escalation occurred on many U.S. college campuses, most notably Kent State where Ohio national guardsmen shot and killed four students. Counter demonstrations by office workers and construction workers voiced support for Nixon.

However, the U.S. Congress responded by rescinding the Tonkin Gulf Resolution of 1964 under which Presidents Johnson and Nixon had conducted military operations in South Vietnam for seven years without a declaration of war by Congress. In addition, the Cooper-Church amendment to the Supplementary Foreign Assistance Act of 1970 barred U.S. ground troops and advisers from participating in military actions in Laos and Cambodia in the future.

The Cooper-Church amendment ignored U.S. Air Force operations in Laos and Cambodia, so air operations in support of Lam Son 719 were allowed. The Army provided heavy artillery shelling across the border in support, but the prohibition against U.S. ground troops participating in or advising South Vietnamese military operations in Laos, as they had in Cambodia, meant this operation would test the readiness of the ARVN to operate effectively by itself in the face of increased U.S. troop withdrawals.

However, the preparation was a mess. ARVN units were not used to conducting large-scale operations of any kind, much less on their own. In an effort to keep the operation secret, individual units that were to participate in the operation were not told until January 17th. The ARVN Airborne Division (the Red Hats), who were to lead the operation, were not told until February 2nd, less than a week before the attack was to begin.

Despite all the efforts to keep the operation secret, the North Vietnamese learned of it in advance and were waiting.

"One of the things that always bothered a lot of Americans throughout our relationship with the South Vietnamese was that there was a feeling of suspicion always that the enemy was in their camp somewhere," said Vaught. "On any number of occasions, American operations, South Vietnamese and American joint operations, and other undertakings were clearly compromised through some form of security lead during the planning phase."

The Vietnamese Airborne Division moved into Laos and occupied a number of designated areas establishing fire bases. Shortly after they were on the ground, the NVA launched some very strong counterattacks against them pushing them out of firebase 31, which included most of one of the light battalions of artillery the Red Hats were using. NVA tanks came charging across the area directly into the firebase. A large battle resulted, but in approximately three hours, the Red Hats had to abandon the firebase, losing much material and equipment to the enemy.

"I was up in the northern area of South Vietnam where a lot of big command posts had been established before returning to my office at Long Binh," said Vaught. "When the operation got underway, it wasn't long before it was in trouble."

After the initial difficulties of the Vietnamese Airborne Division, Vaught received a call at his office from Major General Don Cole, Chief of Staff of the Military Assistance Command – Vietnam (MACV).

"You've been reassigned to be the airborne division advisor," Cole told Vaught. "There's a helicopter on the way to pick you up. Get down here to see General Abrams, then you're going off this afternoon to take over the detachment."

Vaught went to MACV HQ at Tan Son Nhut Air Base near Saigon where he met with Generals Cole and Abrams. Abrams told Vaught the Vietnamese Airborne Division was hard up against the enemy and looked like it was ready to break and run.

"I want you to get them turned around and ready to fight," Abrams said. "You'd better get it done."

"Sir, would you help me please by telling the corps commander what the arrangement is," Vaught responded. "I was up there last week as CDC liaison officer and the command arrangements weren't very well understood. I know I'll need to do some things that are not going to sit too well with the way they're doing business now."

Vaught caught a flight with General Fred Weyand to Quang Tri where he met with General Sullivan, the corps commander, who briefed Vaught on what he knew of the situation. Vaught moved to the advanced corps command post where he received a further briefing from Brigadier General Jackson, and then he was taken over to the Vietnamese Airborne Division command post where he was introduced to Lieutenant General Du Quoc Dong, commander of the ARVN Airborne forces.

"I had a big 1st Cav patch on my right shoulder," Vaught said. "When General Dong saw that he said, 'Ah, the 1st Cavalry is here. Now we will fight.'"

After talking to his advisors in the airborne advisory team, Vaught began to formulate a plan to get the division back into operating status. The division was stopped on a series of firebases, facing strong opposition from NVA units, and not moving. His first recommendation was to get the division moving off the static firebases.

Vaught developed a simple, but effective, coordinated attack formula for extricating units, over the next two days, from firebases that were in close contact with the enemy. This included an arc light strike within 300-500 meters of the firebase followed by a low altitude strike by a squadron of fighter bombers. While the low altitude strike was occurring, helicopters would fly in two fresh companies of infantry and remove the dead and wounded from the units already engaged. After the divisional units moved off the firebases, Vaught had them conduct operations in the jungle.

"I was told it was going to be a disaster to move off the firebases," said Vaught. "It was a grand disaster alright because we never failed to accomplish the missions assigned to us and lost very few people in the process. As a result, we were assigned to be the rear guard as all the troops moved out of Laos."

Along the way, the airborne division had to relieve an armor/infantry task force that was surrounded by NVA units. This included calling in arc-light air strikes to within 500 meters of the friendly units.

"If you've never seen an arc-light strike, it's hard to imagine the devastation it causes, but that's what it took to break the forces surrounding the ARVN troops and get them out of there," Vaught said.

When the armor unit got back to the river boundary separating Laos from Vietnam, the vehicles were almost out of gas. The armor commander proposed abandoning the equipment with the men of the unit fording the river.

Vaught responded, "Disapproved. You stay there and dispose yourself into a tactical formation for defense until you receive further orders."

Vaught contacted the 101st Airborne Division and rounded up all the hook-capable UH-1s in the area to fly fuel to the armor units in 55-gallon drums. He also requested an air cavalry reconnaissance platoon to help find fording locations for the vehicles. Included in the plans were getting four small bulldozers to the area to combine with demolitions in order to reduce the 30-foot bank on the Vietnamese side of the river. Beginning at around 11 p.m., the task force began crossing the river.

"We saved some 360 tanks and armored personnel carriers and all the troops," said Vaught. "It was a great example of what air mobility can do for you and what determined soldiers can accomplish when they decide to get the job done rather than knuckling under and quitting."

One more mission remained when the airborne division was called upon to help another South Vietnamese unit that was being overrun by enemy forces at Dak To. The airborne troops engaged the enemy and kicked their units off the hill they were occupying with large casualties. The airborne units occupied the hill for approximately one week before they were relieved. After that, the division returned to Saigon for an intensive phase of re-equipping, retraining, re-balancing the division, and recruiting more troops.

"We went through an intensive program with new people, and within six to eight weeks, the division was back up to 12,000 personnel again," Vaught said. "I tried to tell the division commander, as best I could, to move quickly with his fellow senior Vietnamese officers to strengthen their respective units to conduct unilateral operations because the American Army is going home."

Looking back on the eventual fall of South Vietnam in 1975, Vaught said he believed the problem was that the South Vietnamese units never learned to facilitate the use of firepower and logistics.

"It's my belief, when the American advisory teams were removed, the logistics system collapsed and the firepower system collapsed," Vaught said. "Nevertheless, I will never forget the valorous conduct of the Vietnamese Airborne Division soldiers and their leaders. It was a tremendously encouraging seven months I spent with the division, and I felt very fulfilled by it."

Colonel James Vaught presenting awards after Lam Son 719 to Vietnamese Paratroopers

Chapter Eleven

At the end of his second Vietnam tour, Vaught was ordered to the 18th Airborne Corps, at Fort Bragg, where he was assigned as commander of the 12th Support Brigade, which would soon be re-designated as Corps Support Command (COSCOM). The brigade was vastly understrength, having about 3,400 soldiers assigned against an authorization of 6,000.

For the next four years, Vaught would wrestle with problems of poor morale and discipline among soldiers, cutbacks on troop numbers and operating funds, and the transition from a wartime to a peacetime force while attempting to keep the operational status of the 18th Airborne Corps and its 82nd Airborne Division at a high level in order to meet contingencies they may be ordered to address. The 82nd Airborne was designated to be one of the first responder units to trouble spots anywhere on the globe. Its battalions rotated in "ready status" for immediate deployment, if necessary. The motto was "wheels up in eighteen hours" from the time orders for deployment were received until troops were on their way.

Vaught said the Army was going through what he called its "coffee house" period in stateside units. Many troops would return, mostly from Vietnam, with between six weeks and six months of active duty obligation remaining. They would be assigned to stateside units to complete their obligated time.

"Their motivation was to do as little as they could, be gone as much as they could, and get out of the Army at the earliest opportunity," Vaught said. "Trying to motivate them to make an effective contribution to the unit was a real challenge."

Vaught said discipline was bad in the stateside units with drugs "all over the place" and soldiers challenging authority. One minor example was the "Haircut Review Board" that Vaught's predecessor had instituted in the brigade. If a soldier didn't want to get his hair cut, he would appeal up through channels to the review board who would hear both sides of the story and decide whether or not the soldier had to cut his hair. Vaught cancelled the Haircut Review Board on his first day as commander.

"That's just an example of how disciplinary infractions had gotten out of hand," said Vaught. "Key personnel at brigade headquarters were wasting time deciding whether some soldier was going to cut his hair or not. The Army publishes standards. You may or may not like them, but you can read and understand them. What the Army says is what we were going to do."

Another measure of discipline, or lack of it, was the uniforms the soldiers were wearing. According to Vaught, when he first got there and had a company fall out they would be in five or six different uniforms.

"They were wearing whatever they wanted," Vaught said. "Some in Class A uniforms, some Class B uniforms, and they were mixing in some civilian clothes and strange looking caps and boots. We got back to authorized uniforms and authorized appearance through daily formations. We got back to standards that the Army expected."

However, the biggest initial problem Vaught and the Army overall faced occurred when the Army tried to inventory its resources as it pulled large numbers of troops out of Vietnam. The brigade received a message to release a certain category of soldiers as the Army was reducing its overall strength by 40,000 by the end of December 1971.

"I got to checking around, and I found out that we were reporting on our morning reports and our strength accounting system more people than we actually had," Vaught said.

Vaught went down to a randomly chosen company and had it fall out. The company had strength authorization of 300, were carrying 250 soldiers on the morning report, but only about 180 soldiers actually mustered. Vaught asked the first sergeant about the discrepancy between the morning report and the actual muster.

The first sergeant said, "Well, they're gone. They're discharged from the Army, but we don't have orders so we can't drop them from the morning report."

Checking with his personnel service company, Vaught found that was the case. The PSC had fallen behind in posting orders, in many cases because soldiers were back from Vietnam, without their service record, to finish their remaining time in the Army.

When reporting into the brigade the soldier would say something like "I'm so and so, here's my last pay stub and here's my orders assigning me here." When asked where his or her service record was the reply would be something like, "Well I turned it in at so and so and they never gave it back to me and they gave me these orders and said to come here and they would mail my service record. I've been in the Army for such and such a time and I'm due to get discharged in x number of weeks and I want to go home."

"There wasn't any point in trying to track the service record because, often, the organization which he had left had been deactivated," said Vaught. "The people in the personnel service company, who were charged with that kind of work, had their term of service expiring too."

Vaught ordered his unit commanders to conduct a muster the next morning and provide an exact number of people who remained on the morning report. "I want a face-to-face physical muster accounting against the morning report, and I'll check it out," Vaught said. "We found out we had about 1,200 soldiers being carried on morning reports who had actually been discharged."

"I took those numbers to General Hay quickly," said Vaught. "The end strength reporting is not getting to the Department of the Army. We're carrying people on the morning report as assigned and present for duty who have already been discharged and are home."

The problem went up the line to the Department of the Army, which sent an order to all units to do a muster, find out who was actually still in the Army, and adjust the morning reports accordingly.

"I ordered every unit in the 12th Support Brigade to make a note on the morning report, for every soldier who couldn't be accounted for in a muster, that they were discharged per order of the brigade commander."

Vaught then published a General Order, which was to be attached to the morning report. The brigade began requisitioning against the shortages, and by Spring 1972, it was back up to approximately eighty percent of authorized strength.

It quickly became apparent to Vaught that there was a need to reorganize logistical support arrangements so the brigade could actually support the 18th Airborne Corps and its contingency plans. A support brigade from Fort Devens, Massachusetts, a movements control center from Fort Lee, New Jersey, and a mobile computer system from Fort Lewis, Washington were all moved to Fort Bragg. All were integrated into the 12th Support Brigade in a complete reorganization. By June 1972, the brigade was re-designated as 1st COSCOM. Specific missions were assigned to each unit so the unit knew what to do both in support of troop units at Fort Bragg and throughout the corps for participation in contingency operations wherever the corps and its elements were sent.

The brigade was missing training manuals, and Vaught solved that problem by establishing an Military Occupational Specialty (MOS) library. This made it possible for soldiers to come in and study in preparation for MOS tests upon which their promotion depended. Within the individual units, local-level training on the field manual was conducted so that each company knew what it was supposed to do.

In addition, Vaught got missions assigned for COSCOM where the brigade got involved in supplying Fort Bragg. This included receiving supplies at the Knox Street Warehouse and making sure the supplies got to where they were supposed to go, just as they would have to do in time of war.

"Up until that time, the brigade was supplying people as warm bodies to go somewhere and work for somebody else," said Vaught. "You don't build leadership and you don't build field organizations by sending your soldiers off every day to work for somebody else."

Vaught's philosophy as COSCOM commander was as follows:
1. Give the soldiers a challenge with something they have been trained to do.
2. Help them do it better, and let them see they are a vital part of the unit.
3. Promote those who are performing well, and take corrective action with those who aren't.

"I tried to stabilize the officers and the NCOs, but there was a lot of turbulence in the Army in those days no matter what you did," said Vaught. "We started in bad circumstances, but as we built the unit, we built pride."

In June 1973, Vaught was promoted to Brigadier General and was re-assigned as Chief of Staff of the 18th Airborne Corps. It was a time of change at the top of the 18th Airborne Corps as General John Hay (the corps commander) was retiring at the end of the month and the Chief of Staff Vaught would be relieving him; General "Brick" Krause had orders to Korea.

"I was in my quarters at about 7 a.m. when I got a call from General Hay," Vaught said. "He said, 'congratulations, you've been selected for brigadier general, and you're going to be the corps Chief of Staff. You've got to get up here and learn what's going on and run the corps until General Seitz (Hay's relief) gets here.'"

While at COSCOM, Vaught had reviewed corps contingency plans from a logistics standpoint, ensuring units had adequate supplies to perform contingency missions. He had built a readiness, recording, and reporting system that he carried forward to the full corps as Chief of Staff. The readiness room at corps headquarters was manual. Tags were made up for each unit mounted on a big board. Colors green, yellow, or red were used to indicate the readiness of each unit.

"One of the things I was confronted with when I became Chief of Staff was trying to resolve a shortage of $15 million that we needed to complete the fiscal year," said Vaught. "If I couldn't get that resolved we would not have had adequate supplies to ensure the 82nd Airborne Division and other units would have all the things they needed to have to participate in any contingency situations."

"The challenge to leadership, to operations officers, supply officers, staff, and the chain of command is to identify a management program that will best use funds available to optimally let the organization train and do what they have to do to execute a mission," Vaught said.

Vaught said he learned early on to frontload use of funds in order to accomplish goals. With the approval of the corps commander, the corps and its individual units were trained and ready to accomplish any objectives assigned to them.

In October 1974, Vaught was reassigned as Assistant Division Commander, Support, of the 82nd Airborne Division.

"When I was assigned to the 82nd, the division commander and both assistant division commanders were preparing to leave at about the same time," Vaught said. "General Seitz felt that someone with experience at the corps level was needed to provide some continuity in the 82nd."

Having spent three years already at Fort Bragg, Vaught was familiar with the installation in general and COSCOM in particular.

"I found the division was not taking full advantage of the services available from COSCOM and the installation," Vaught said. "They were trying to do everything themselves as much as possible."

Vaught was with one of the rifle companies one morning when rifles were being issued for an unannounced readiness drill. Approximately ten soldiers ended up with no rifle because fifteen rifles had already been turned in for repair and another fifteen did not work.

"I did some checking to see if this was a normal case," said Vaught. "I checked another couple of units and found similar problems. Overall, there were approximately 1,200 rifles that needed repair."

Vaught found there were seventeen qualified armorers in the maintenance battalion, but only six were actually working on rifle repair. The remaining armorers were somewhere else performing other duties.

"We got them all back working on rifles and monitored the situation until it was cleared up," Vaught said.

A similar situation was found with other material to the point that the ready battalion often had to borrow equipment from another battalion in order to be fully ready for a mission if called.

"That's bad for the mission and for the Army," said Vaught. "If we can't be ready in a mission short of war, what in the world will we do when a war does occur?"

Vaught said a battalion should not have to borrow from another battalion. In an installation the size of Fort Bragg, it was his opinion that there is sufficient equipment on the base to meet any shortfalls. If a battalion falls short of something, it should come down automatically from COSCOM or the installation.

Vaught reprioritized responsibilities. One example was physical training (PT). Initially everybody in the division would fall out and do PT at the same time, and it would be 0900 or later before anyone showed up in the maintenance shops and other support facilities.

"The first area of responsibility of a support organization is to provide support," Vaught said. "It's more important to have the M-16 rifles ready for deployment than have the soldiers in the rifle repair section doing morning PT. PT can be done in the afternoons after the work is done or can be made an individual responsibility in extreme situations."

Analysts often criticize the Army for having operators plan in a vacuum that does not consider many of the support aspects of a contingency or operation plan. In order to negate this problem, Vaught and Brigadier General Jack Forrest, Assistant Division Commander, Maneuver, met daily to coordinate their respective areas of responsibility.

"I went to the field a lot, down with the rifle companies," Vaught said. "Jack had a standing invitation to visit any of the support units at any time to make sure we were doing everything he thought was necessary to support his maneuver and operations concepts."

After approximately one year as ADC of the 82nd Airborne Division, Vaught was promoted to Major General and expected orders to command a division. Instead, he was chosen to head to Izmir, Turkey as Chief of Staff, Allied Land Forces Southeastern Europe.

"I had been promised a division," said Vaught. "But General Melvin Zais, the Land Southeast commander, called and told me he had a staff problem in Izmir and needed my help straightening it out. So, off I went to Turkey."

Col Vaught's Pass and Review at 1st Corps Support Command (COSCOM) in 1972

Chapter Twelve

When Vaught assumed the duties of Chief of Staff of Allied Land Forces, Southeastern Europe, he stepped into a sticky situation among NATO Allies but also into one of the oldest areas of recorded European history.

The headquarters is located in Izmir, a major port and one of the largest cities on Turkey's west coast, along the Aegean Sea and 150 miles south of the Dardanelles. Greek settlers can be traced to the area as far back as the 3rd Millennium BC. Izmir was known as Smyrna in ancient times. The settlement was destroyed by war in 600 BC and rebuilt by Alexander the Great in the 4th Century BC. During the Crusades to the Holy Land in the 14th Century, Izmir was invaded and occupied by the Knights of Rhodes.

Virtually every Russian ruler since Peter the Great (1682 – 1721) sought to conquer warm water ports for the Russian navy. Their eyes were constantly focused on Constantinople (Istanbul), the Dardanelles, and the Bosporus Straits from the Black Sea to the Aegean Sea and into the Mediterranean Sea. This desire led to several conflicts in the Crimea as well as the occupation of Constantinople and Smyrna after World War I until the occupiers were expelled in 1922, which led to the rise of the Turkish Republic under Mustafa Kemal Atatürk. The Soviet Union demanded military bases in the Turkish Straits after World War II, which led to the Truman Doctrine in 1947. The doctrine declared the intentions of the United States to guarantee the security of both Greece and Turkey with large-scale military and economic support. Both countries were included in the Marshall Plan after World War II and were welcomed into the NATO alliance in 1952. This became the southeastern border of NATO with the headquarters in Izmir responsible for land defense of both Turkey and Greece.

LANDSOUTHEAST, as it is known in NATO, is responsible for deterring all forms of aggression along the Turkish Straits, eastern Thrace, and Turkey's southern border and eastern frontier. It is co-located with the Sixth Allied Tactical Air Force whose mission is to ensure full-time air defense of Turkey.

Greece and Turkey have had periods of mutual hostility and reconciliation since Greece won its independence from the Ottoman Empire in 1821. This history has caused repeated tensions between the two countries, which also found their way into the headquarters of the Allied Land Forces Southeastern Europe.

One year before Vaught was sent to Turkey, Greece and Turkey had fought a war over Cyprus. The island had been a matter of conflict in Greek-Turkish relations since the 1950s. The Greek-Cypriot population share of the island's total population was eighty-two percent causing several attempts to cede Cyprus to Greece. In 1960, Great Britain awarded Cyprus independence from its empire with Greek and Turkish troops stationed on the island to protect their respective communities.

In July 1974, a band of Greek-Cypriot nationalists, backed by the military junta then governing Greece, staged a coup against Cypriot President Archbisop Makarios, replacing him as president with Nikos Sampson. In response, Turkey invaded Cyprus, occupying the northern thirty-seven percent of the island and expelling Greek-Cypriots from this area. Sampson's coup collapsed a few days later, and the Greek military junta fell from power before the end of the month for failing to confront the Turkish invasion. However, the Turks remained in occupation of the claimed section of Cyprus.

As a result of the 1974 Cyprus incident, Greece withdrew its portion of the Allied Land Forces Southeastern Europe headquarters complement. Approximately eighty percent of the headquarters staff was made up of Greeks and Turks with approximately forty percent of that amount being Greek. The remaining twenty percent of the staff was made up of American, British, and Italian personnel. By the time Vaught arrived, the headquarters was considerably understaffed due to the Greek withdrawal. A further complication was an embargo, for political reasons, by the United States against shipping weapons to Turkey after the Cyprus invasion. In response, Turkey cut off authority for the United States to bring supplies into Turkey and cut off the customs entry points into the area. A key southeastern border area between NATO and the Soviet Union was threatened by centuries old rivalries between Greece and Turkey and political considerations back in Washington, D.C.

"We had bilateral agreements with Turkey and agreements within the NATO umbrella," said Vaught. "How we could bring ourselves to invoke an embargo on an ally in a common undertaking was a mystery to me. We were literally running out of food and everything else by Christmas time in 1975."

General Zais was able to exert personal influence on the Turkish military and government to get some relief on the supply issue by Christmas. The Turkish military equipment was, for the most part, obsolete. Most of the elements of the Army were equipped with vintage equipment from World War II and the Korean War. Efforts had been made to get equipment from the Vietnam War buildup that the U.S. Army was replacing turned over to the Turkish Army.

"Some will say the Turkish Army was less well supported than any other large member of NATO," said Vaught.

During Vaught's tenure in Turkey, the main thrust of work was on contingency plans.

"We got good cooperation out of the Turkish officers," said Vaught. "They weren't as well trained on staff work as we would have liked, but they were very willing to learn and made a very significant contribution."

During the time Vaught was at LANDSOUTHEAST, General Zais commanded until May 1976, followed by General William Knowlton for just over a year, and then by General Sam Walker. During Walker's tenure, reorganization was made to make Turkish participation and responsibilities more effective after the loss of the Greek contingent.

"One of the proposals was that the position of commander of LANDSOUTHEAST should be changed from a U.S. national to a Turkish national," said Vaught. "It was apparent that the Greeks weren't going to come back, and most of the Turkish combat forces were assigned to NATO primarily to defend Turkish territory."

Perfection of contingency plans, visits to subordinate headquarters, and observation of frequent field exercises took most of Vaught's time, but it was his ability to build close relationships with subordinates, increase training and performance, and build an 'esprit de corps' among his staff that was most valuable.

Despite the political and military problems faced during his time at LANDSOUTHEAST, Vaught's contributions did not go unnoticed by his superiors. In addition to getting 30 out of 30 with a recommendation for immediate promotion in his fitness report, Vaught received the following comments from General Knowlton, endorsed by General Alexander Haig, Supreme Allied Commander Europe:

Major General Vaught has performed superbly in the many facets of his role as Chief of Staff in this International Headquarters. The headquarters building is in the city of Izmir, while our sister HQ, SIXTH ATAF, is about a 20 minute drive away. A half hour outside the city is a vast underground headquarters from which we operate in crises or exercises. A Joint Signal Support Group supports all three activities. All this is done without 20 percent of the authorized staff who are Greek and who departed in the summer of 1974. One further point about the staff is that the Turkish officers who are assigned do not attend a special course or language instruction before arrival – as they do for all other NATO assignments. This makes the Chief of Staff perform two duties which lead in different directions: creating a smooth-running headquarters, while training and educating a Turkish staff component which is On the Job Training." General Vaught rapidly gained the confidence of his Turkish deputy and of the Turkish officers. Under his guidance, staff work improved in quality while formal and informal training for Turkish staff officers was instituted. The Turkish response to this has been outstanding; the percentage of international meetings away from Izmir where Turks have represented this headquarters has doubled under General Vaught's sure tutelage. A large number of briefings which used to be given by American or British officers are now given in English by Turkish officers. The result has been a closeness of bond among officers of different nationalities and an increasing effectiveness of cooperation at a time when other elements of the Turkish military are less disposed to cooperate with the U.S. Turkish officers find the dual nature of this staff so useful that a record number have applied for extension in order to continue their staff development. When Major General Vaught arrived, the political difficulties between the U.S. and Turkey, the departure of the Greeks, the restrictions placed upon the American community and what they consider normal life in a foreign country - - all of these combined to present Major General Vaught with a real challenge. In two years, he has pulled this staff together into a cooperative, enthusiastic team. Only a year ago, the environment in the JCOC of the underground headquarters showed a division between Air Force and Army and a reluctance to expand the international contributions to solutions during exercises. Major General Vaught has done an absolutely superb job in an international staff position beset with political and military problems. At the same time, he has had to guide closely the affairs of this military community in a period when Turkish intransigence has made life for U.S. military families very difficult. An exceptional administrator, staff director and tactician, with an empathy for the practical side of life, he should be given command of a division upon leaving this assignment. It is my belief that he will be the outstanding division commander in the Army during the period of such service.

General Knowlton's comments, with General Haig's concurrence, proved to be true as Vaught was assigned to take command of the newly established 24th Infantry Division at Fort Stewart, Georgia in September 1977.

Major General Vaught in Turkey, May 1976

Chapter Thirteen

The 24th Infantry Division traces its lineage to the Hawaiian Division formed at Schofield Barracks, Oahu in 1921. In the Fall of 1941, the Hawaiian Division assets were split to form two divisions with Hawaiian Division headquarters being re-designated Headquarters, 24th Infantry Division.

The division saw heavy fighting in the Pacific Theater during World War II, beginning at New Guinea and driving through the Philippine Islands, liberating those territories from occupying Japanese forces. After the armistice, the 24th Division was part of the occupying force in Japan. When hostilities broke out in Korea with North Korean forces invading South Korea in June 1950, the 24th Division was the first unit to respond after President Truman ordered U.S. ground forces into Korea. For the first eighteen months of the Korean War, the 24th Division was heavily engaged against both North Korean and Chinese forces, suffering a total of 10,000 casualties during that period. It was withdrawn to reserve force to rest and replenish its numbers, but it returned to Korea for patrol duty after the end of major combat operations.

The division was relocated to Augsburg, Germany on July 1, 1958. The 24th Division remained in Germany until 1968 when its First and Second Brigades were redeployed to Fort Riley, Kansas with the Third Brigade remaining in Germany. As the Army began its withdrawal from Vietnam in 1970 with a resultant reduction in forces, the 24th Division was inactivated in April 1970.

In September 1975, the 24th Division was reactivated at Fort Stewart, Georgia as part of a new program to build a 16-division U.S. Army force. With the force reductions after the end of combat operations in Vietnam and the anti-military hangover from that war, the division was still in the process of attempting to get to full strength when Vaught assumed command of the division in September 1977.

"General Rosenbloom had gone there as a brigadier general when the division was really only a brigade slice," Vaught said. "He was promoted just as it was converted to full division status and had done an outstanding job bringing it to that point. I got there just after that time, and there was a lot of construction as the post was being converted to a division post."

In addition to being reactivated as a division, the 24th Division was in the process of being converted to a mechanized division.

"When I got there, the two armor battalions were just being activated in the 2nd Brigade, and there were three infantry battalions in the 1st Brigade with no armor," Vaught said. "The 1st Brigade had had enough time to get itself pretty well postured and trained, and it was in a good readiness status."

However, the 2nd Brigade had suffered from personnel resources being taken out of the pipeline, according to Vaught, and the division staff tried to protect the 1st Brigade and perpetuate it into a combat ready organization. He talked to Forces Command (FORSCOM) for clarification on their expectations for the division.

"FORSCOM said it was alright to keep 1st Brigade in the highest readiness status that could be achieved with the resources available, but the overriding mission was to get the entire division activated and begin to balance all units to make sure the division itself became a unitized, ready force," Vaught said.

Vaught said the quality of troops in the 2nd Brigade, especially the non-commissioned officers, was markedly below what it was in the 1st Brigade.

"I had a difficult decision to make of either getting rid of those that were markedly below what I desired, hoping I would get better quality coming through the pipeline, or moving people out of the 1st Brigade to the 2nd, bringing down the readiness of the 1st," Vaught said. "We had the same types of difficulties in the artillery and other parts of the post."

In addition to the two regular Army brigades, the 48th Brigade of the Georgia National Guard was assigned as the roundout brigade to bring the division up to full manning. Vaught scheduled a meeting with Gov. George Busbee of Georgia and the Adjutant General of Georgia.

Gov. Busbee told Vaught he was counting on him to tell the 48th Brigade what it had to do in order to meet the expectations of the Army. Vaught said the governor told him if the Georgia contingent was not supporting the 24th Division and if there was anything Vaught needed, he was to tell the governor.

"He came and visited the unit when it was in the field, and he visited my headquarters every two or three months," Vaught said. "We had a tremendous rapport with the governor and the Adjutant General."

However, in the post-Vietnam era, even in the Deep South, it was not always easy for the military to recruit.

"The Georgia National Guard was losing a lot of people, and they were having trouble recruiting new members," Vaught said. "A lot of their units were understrength. We helped them with our recruiters and the governor pitched in with support and by 1979, the 48th Brigade was at something like 104% of authorized strength."

While strength was rising through recruiting efforts, Vaught combined training between the 1st Brigade and the 48th Brigade.

"I wanted a counterpart relationship between units of the 1st Brigade and units of the 48th Brigade," Vaught said. "We took A Company of the 19th Infantry and hooked it up with A Company of one of the infantry battalions in the Guard and did that right down through the Brigade. It was in the interest of both to be trained and ready to go."

When the Guard members came to Fort Stewart for training, they were matched with their counterpart sponsoring regular Army unit to ensure all training was completed. As the division moved more into mechanized units, the process worked in reverse, according to Vaught.

"The 48th had a lot of old timers in it, and they had a maintenance facility at Fort Stewart, which had been there a long time," Vaught said. "As we introduced armor and mech into the 24th Division and started to learn how to maintain it and shoot, we found out there were people in the 48th Brigade who knew a lot more about those MOSs (military occupational specialties) than our regular Army people did. They sent people to help us learn how to drive tanks and maintain the armored personnel carriers. It wasn't a one-way street; we helped them train, and they helped us train. We didn't have any rigid lines of separation. That brigade was part of the 24th Division."

In order to motivate and train the soldiers, Vaught stressed the first responsibility of any unit is to be very good at whatever its TO&E (table of organization and equipment) name is.

"If your name is mechanized infantry battalion, you spend most of your effort being the best mechanized infantry battalion in the Army," said Vaught. "That's what you're going to get graded on by me."

Vaught stressed that specific type of training for the morning and required everybody to be there. Other types of training, such as fitting gas masks or instruction on the Geneva Convention, were scheduled for the afternoon. People could be excused from afternoon instruction for things like meetings at battalion headquarters, but all officers and men had to attend basic unit training in the morning.

"You'd be amazed at the difference that makes when everyone understands they are supposed to be training and executing their primary Table of Organization and Equipment (TO&E) mission during the prime hours of the duty day," Vaught said. "I made it my business to get up early in the morning to where the units were – in mess halls, motor pools, firing ranges, and training areas. I showed up where I could see whether the leadership was there. If some subordinate commander wanted to see me, he had to find me in the field because that's where I was until at least noontime."

Vaught said most people in the Army are going to work for you and help you on the primary job in the prime hours of the first part of the day if you've got something interesting and challenging for them to do.

"If you start later, aren't very well organized, and don't put emphasis in the right place, they'll drift off to something else," Vaught said.

Vaught said an open-door policy, which allowed complaints and suggestions from the ranks, was important, but had to be handled properly.

"For most of the personal problems or training problems of the enlisted soldiers, I believed that was the sergeant's business," Vaught said. "I insisted that the command sergeant major, other sergeant majors, or the sergeant major of the IG handle that. One of the systems I instituted at Fort Bragg and continued at other places was to take a well-respected non-commissioned officer in my IG section and have him talk directly to every enlisted soldier that came to the IG. You'd be amazed at the number of problems, or so-called problems, that got solved."

In addition to commanding the 24th Division, Vaught had responsibilities for the Ranger battalion stationed at Fort Stewart.

"When I went through orientation at FORSCOM headquarters, General Kroesen, the FORSCOM Commander, told me that General Cavazos at Fort Lewis, Washington and I at Fort Stewart were directly responsible to him for ensuring the readiness of the Ranger units," Vaught said. "There was a Ranger unit at each of our posts, and he expected us to take a personal interest in them. In addition to that, if any type of contingencies came up, I was the prospective commander for the contingency force until such time that REDCOM (Readiness Command at Fort McDill, Florida) either deployed it or chopped it out."

Immediately after arriving at Fort Stewart, Vaught began looking at the Ranger battalion. He found it quite a bit understrength.

"The companies were at about 50% of authorized strength in the field," Vaught said. "A Ranger company can do a lot of things, but it can do a hell of a lot more if it's at authorized strength. When you cut the rifle strength markedly, you are cutting your operating strength drastically."

One month after Vaught arrived at Fort Stewart, the Ranger unit was called up for a contingency drill. The unit was given the task of conducting a drill that would end up in Fort McCoy, Wisconsin. The drill included taking over an aircraft that had been seized by terrorists and included hostages. The Ranger unit was given the mission of moving across the country, assaulting the airplane, and releasing the hostages.

"I was very disappointed in the planning and execution all the way through the mission," said Vaught. "It was very apparent that the Ranger unit was not only understrength, but also not adequately trained for this type of mission. I found myself in the position of higher headquarters expecting us to be capable to do something that, clearly, we were not trained and ready to do."

When the unit arrived back at Fort Stewart, Vaught put in a call to FORSCOM to recommend what he felt was needed to correct the problems.

"I got authorization to take the battalion out of the contingency plan cycle for ninety days to get them retrained and back up and ready to go again," Vaught said. "We went into a very intensive training program. We started the RIP (Ranger Indoctrination Program) that would take new personnel sent as replacements through a three-week intensive course before they went to the battalion. It was useful because we could screen out people who obviously weren't going to qualify to be in the battalion."

Included in the training were at least fifteen jumps before the replacements joined a Ranger company.

"I've always thought the Army's kidded itself by saying they've got a trained parachutist after five jumps," Vaught said. "He may be a qualified parachutist when he comes out of parachute school at Fort Benning, but that's all he is. He knows how to jump out of an airplane, but as far as him being a real competent, self-confident airborne soldier, he is not. It's up to the unit to make him that."

Of the required fifteen additional jumps, about half were night jumps out of both airplanes and helicopters. The most competent veterans were put into the field to critique the jumpers and help them improve their skills. Extra voluntary jumping was encouraged on the weekends so that the soldiers became very confident day and night jumpers out of both airplanes and helicopters.

"In this way, the most worrisome part of an airborne operation, the physical act of jumping and landing, became less of a consideration, and we were able to concentrate on mission performance, which is what it's all about," Vaught said. "No matter what you do, a parachute is a pretty lousy means of transportation. But, recognizing that it is one of those skills that Rangers are expected to be very good at, they ought to be very good at it."

In addition to parachute skills and techniques, the RIP platoon period was an intensive time of physical training and introduction and review of skills that the men should know when they got into a unit. When a man finished the RIP platoon and was sent to an operational unit, the unit knew it was getting a qualified man ready to go to work.

"We trained the entire battalion as a unit," Vaught said. "At the end of the 90-day training period, the 1st Ranger Battalion was second to none in the Army. People who observed them were confident the battalion could accomplish an assigned mission."

In addition to developing training and overseeing basic soldiering skills, Vaught completed the work of building and converting the division to a mechanized division and oversaw considerable construction as the post transitioned from one that housed a brigade to a full division.

"I used the Association of the U.S. Army, as well as my public affairs office, as vehicles for coordinating, sponsoring, and getting community involvement," said Vaught. "I also picked a very competent lieutenant colonel as my G-5. He was my primary liaison between the community and my office."

Vaught said he assigned brigade commanders community responsibility.

"I did it for two reasons," he said. "One was to decentralize my responsibilities. The second was to get my colonels involved. They thought they were getting a dirty deal at first, but they came to enjoy it. If you talked to them now, I believe they would tell you some of the most enjoyable moments in their career was getting to know the people in the community around Fort Stewart."

After two years commanding the 24th Division, Vaught was reassigned as Director of Operations, Readiness and Mobilization for the Deputy Chief of Staff of the Army for Operations.

Major General Vaught in Fort Stewart, GA 1976-1978

Chapter Fourteen

The United States Army was a latecomer into the counterterrorism business. The British Special Air Service was the original military counterterrorism unit and remains the standard to which all others compare themselves. The SAS originated in World War II from an idea of British Captain David Stirling. It began as a desert raiding force created to weaken the logistics and air operations associated with the German Afrika Corps. The SAS also operated in occupied Europe as a raiding unit that parachuted into enemy territory ambushing German units and attacking railways and trains.

It was disbanded after the war but revived in 1947 and reorganized in 1952. The 22nd SAS Regiment is the British Regular Army unit that conducts offensive operations, counter-revolutionary warfare, counterterrorism, close protection, and defense diplomacy missions. When paramilitary and civilian terrorist groups such as Black September and the Baader-Meinhoff Gang began hijacking airplanes and bombing military installations in the early 1970s, the SAS modified its training to include emphasis on counterterrorism. Germany and France joined Britain in concentrating on counterterrorist operations with the establishment of the GSG-9 and GIGN, respectively, but the United States waited another five years until the 1st Special Forces Operational Detachment-DELTA was formed in 1977 under the command of Colonel Charles Beckwith.

Beckwith was a unique character, obstinate, arrogant, opinionated, and not well suited to operating within the military chain of command. He had received some training with 22nd SAS early in his career and had become familiar with the thoughts of British Field Marshal Sir William Slim. Field Marshall Slim believed that a special operations force that was able to penetrate deep into enemy territory, collaborate with indigenous citizens, collect intelligence, sabotage enemy installations, and assassinate enemy leaders was an indispensable unit for modern warfare.

After his training with SAS, Beckwith had written a report contrasting British special operations forces with the more traditionally oriented American Special Forces. Beckwith argued for the Army to adopt the British philosophy and training. A few in the Army Special Forces community agreed with Beckwith's conclusions, but many disagreed and he was thrown out of a number of offices manned by more senior officers.

In 1965, Beckwith was given command of an experimental Special Forces unit of thirty men called Project Delta, named after the letter in the Greek alphabet. The unit's mission was to conduct operational and strategic reconnaissance in areas of Vietnam that had long been under the control of the Viet Cong and to direct air strikes into these areas. Other smaller operations included hunter/killer missions, abduction and interrogation of Viet Cong and North Vietnamese Army personnel, bugging compounds and offices, laying minefields, and conducting counterintelligence operations. The unit was to focus on enemy base areas and infiltration routes in the border areas operating with South Vietnamese Army units and the indigenous Nungs. Project Delta was considered one of the most successful Special Forces operations during the Vietnam War.

After American military involvement in the Vietnam War ended in 1972, Special Forces concepts and units became almost an afterthought in traditional Army doctrine. When the Baader-Meinhof Gang bombed an officer's club in Frankfurt, Germany and the headquarters building of U.S. Army Europe in Heidelberg in 1972, Beckwith began lobbying for an American military counterterrorist unit. With the help of successive Army Chiefs of Staff General Bernard Rogers and General "Shy" Meyer, Beckwith was successful in establishing the 1st Special Forces Operational Detachment-DELTA. Its mission was to become the first U.S. military counterterrorism force able to respond to a terrorist crisis anywhere in the world at a moment's notice.

Beginning with a small cadre of Special Forces veterans from the Vietnam War, Beckwith combed regular Army units for volunteers. Special Forces was considered a "dead end" career field at the time, so volunteers were hard to come by and passing the initial selection course was even more difficult. Of the 118 volunteers who began the first selection course, nineteen were accepted into Delta. Eleven more were added from the second selection course. After initial selection, the men trained for nineteen more weeks in marksmanship, room-clearing, close-quarters battle, hostage management, forced entry at crisis points, demolitions, surveillance operations, the collection of intelligence, and much more.

While this type of counterterrorist military training was going on, the concept of Delta was to remain secret. Delta operators were trained to move into an area quietly, often taking commercial flights in groups of two and three. When the unit was in place where a terrorist situation was in the process, Delta would work with local officials, police, and military to take down the terrorists and free the hostages. When the crisis had been brought to a successful conclusion, Delta would fade from the scene in the same way it had come in and return to its base. There would be no headlines, ceremonies, or awards—just the knowledge of a job well done. The Delta unit was so secret that its personnel did not show up on regular Army records.

The Delta troops became very proficient in taking down terrorists and rescuing hostages from hijacked airliners and buildings. After two years of selection and training, Delta consisted of less than 200 men when the unit was scheduled for its final evaluation from November 1-3, 1979. The three-day test was designed to test individual skills as well as dual takedown scenarios of an airliner and a building. When the tests and after action analysis were completed in the early hours of November 4, 1979, Delta was certified as the operational counterterrorist unit in the U.S. Army.

Vaught as Director of Operations, Readiness, and Mobilization and Deputy Chief of Staff for Operations for the Department of the Army oversaw the final certification of Delta. With his connections in place from his recent tenure as Commanding Officer of the 24th Infantry Division, Vaught arranged for the final certification tests to be held at Fort Stewart, Georgia. The hot wash for the exercise was held in a motel near the base beginning in the late hours of November 3, 1979, Vaught's 53rd birthday.

"I rated them a B-minus, which Charlie Beckwith didn't like very much, but I felt Delta was lacking in some of the basic skills of soldiering, things I would not have stood for if they worked for me," Vaught said. "They were certainly skilled in marksmanship, demolitions, and forced entry into areas which contained hostages and terrorists, but they were lacking in a lot of the little things that make a top-notch soldier."

Early on the morning of November 4, 1979, word came back to Washington, D.C. that Iranian students had stormed the walls of the U.S. Embassy in Tehran and taken control of the embassy compound with sixty-three American embassy personnel being held as hostages. Delta was about to get its first experience with a real-time mission as it was chosen to be a part of the Army's contribution to a Joint Task Force to rescue the hostages. The unit was immediately ordered to proceed to the CIA's training facility known as "The Farm."

No command existed within the military structure to conduct special operations of the type that would be needed if the President ordered a military rescue of the hostages from Iran. However, the movement of Delta to The Farm was a first step to begin planning on a contingency basis in case such a mission was eventually ordered.

Vaught returned to his duties at the Pentagon. He was scheduled to make a tour of defense facilities in Western Europe to inspect forward placement of equipment that would be needed in the event of war with the Soviet Union. Vaught arrived in London on Sunday, November 11th, Veterans Day, on the first stop of the trip. He had arranged to stay at his brother-in-law's house in London, within two blocks of the American Embassy, for the first couple of nights while he met with military personnel attached to the Embassy before beginning his inspection tour.

"I arrived in the evening, London time," Vaught said. "During dinner, a phone call came through from General Glenn Otis, my boss in the Pentagon. He ordered me to proceed back to Washington by the quickest means possible."

Vaught's brother-in-law had connections with the CEO of British Airways who arranged for Vaught to have a seat on the Concord leaving Heathrow Airport at 9:00 a.m. London time or 0900 hours Zulu in military parlance.

"I arrived back in New York at 8:30 a.m. local time (1230 Zulu). With the time change and the speed of the Concord, I arrived before I left on local time," Vaught said. "I caught a shuttle to Washington and met with General Meyer at 11:00 a.m. He gave me a quick briefing of what was being planned and took me to the Pentagon to meet General David Jones, Chairman of the Joint Chiefs."

Joint special operations, those that required units from more than one of the military services, were traditionally commanded by a member of the service component that would have the major part in the mission. Meyer designated Vaught to be the overall Commander of a Joint Task Force that would plan and carry out a rescue attempt of the hostages. Other articles and books written about the hostage rescue attempt have left the impression that Beckwith was in charge of the mission. He was not. Beckwith commanded Delta, which would be the force to go into the embassy grounds in Tehran and extract the hostages, but other elements were part of the overall task force. Army Rangers as well as Air Force, Navy, and Marine personnel and equipment were also part of the overall planning for the rescue.

After meeting with General Jones and receiving verbal mission orders and basic operating guidelines, in his new office at the Joint Chiefs of Staff Special Operations Division (JCS/SOD), Vaught asked for an update of the hostage situation and a briefing on planning options to date. A skeleton group of planners had been operating in the SOD for several days already, but the planning process included little in the way of real options. The primary recommendation was for a direct assault by Delta on the embassy with the operation being launched from eastern Turkey with Army CH-47 Chinook helicopters providing the transport. Other options had Delta parachuting in, being trucked overland, or infiltrated from the sea. Vaught pressed the two briefers—an Army colonel and Air Force lieutenant colonel—for meaningful intelligence on the situation, only to learn that nightly television broadcasts from Tehran were the best source available at the time. Nobody had any information as to what was going on inside the embassy or other buildings in the 27-acre embassy complex.

Vaught was extremely unhappy with the lack of intelligence and the planning options that had been discussed. He immediately took charge by saying that planning would go back to square one.

"The military was unprepared to undertake this type of mission," Vaught said. "Special Forces units had been on the decline since Vietnam and Delta had just been certified. There were no aircraft trained or designed to do the type of insertion we would need or any other support units ready to go. We literally had to start from scratch to put together a force to do the job."

As selective and well trained as Delta was, it was not prepared to undertake a mission of this type. Delta had trained for terrorist takedowns and hostage rescue in permissive environments where the local authorities and military provided aid in the form of intelligence, planning, and on-site operations. This was not the case in Iran where the hostages were being held in a city of five million people nearly 1,000 miles into a country where the ruling regime of Iran's leader Ayatollah Khomeini and most of the country's citizens were extremely hostile to the United States. The students that had taken over the embassy and hostile crowds that had been demonstrating outside meant there was certainly not going to be a permissive environment in which Delta could operate.

Vaught's response to the briefing provided the basis for what would be undertaken in the coming months.

"First and foremost, total surprise is the only hope we have for success," he told his staff. "The Iranians have to be convinced we are not going to use military force, so they'll relax their security around the embassy. Then, and only then, we might be able to insert Delta and get them into the compound undetected for a surprise takedown."

Nevertheless, President Carter had ordered General Jones to plan a rescue mission, and Vaught was the man chosen to accomplish that planning and mission.

"The President is the Commander in Chief of the armed forces," Vaught said. "When he gives an order, you go to work. You don't sit around making excuses on why it can't be done; you get it done."

Vaught stressed to his staff the urgency to develop a workable rescue plan as soon as possible. He directed them to concentrate on sound, logical tactics and to make sure that every option proposed must have a means to recover if things go wrong. He also assured the staff that the mission would be sound before it was launched.

"You will not be pressured by anybody to go off half-cocked on a rescue attempt not properly planned," he said. "When we go, it will be with people fully trained and rehearsed in a plan that we all sincerely believe has the best possible chance of success. If anybody tries to put the pressure on you to do otherwise, I want to know about it."

Vaught ordered that all questions from senior officers outside the task force concerning what was going on inside the task force be directed to him.

"You only have to satisfy one general – me," Vaught told his staff.

He then set down guidelines for the staff, "Work starts at 0700 each morning and goes until I say we quit each night." Understanding that the staff was in its infant stages, Vaught also asked staff members for any recommendations they had for highly qualified people who could be brought into the JTF to assist the planning, but he was to make the final decision on their inclusion.

Major General Vaught consults with rescue team forces in 1980

Chapter Fifteen

With Vaught now in place as the task force commander, his first job was to build a task force. In recent years, Vaught had performed well as the JTF commander in several counterterrorism field training exercises including hostage situations. He had organized and been present at the validation exercises for Delta. Now he would be doing the job for real.

For the first week after the hostages were taken, the Unconventional Warfare Branch of the Joint Chiefs of Staff Special Operations Division had been wrestling with the hostage crisis under the direction of Army Colonel Jerry King, a former Special Forces battalion commander and Ranger. Assisted by a representative from the Air Force and Navy as well as an intelligence specialist, King and his small group had spent the week with operational planning, putting together briefing books and developing a preliminary rescue plan.

The organizational structure was that of a Joint Unconventional Warfare Task Force (JUWTF) with Vaught as the overall commander and each service included providing a commander to manage its personnel assigned to the task force. Cooperation of all the services involved to support the JTF commander is absolutely essential for this type of task force to be successful. Unfortunately, at least since World War II, inter-service bickering had sometimes caused problems for the overall effectiveness of such a task force. This would become a problem down the line for Vaught and the Iran task force.

It must also be pointed out that while Vaught had overall command responsibility for the task force, reporting to the Chairman of the JCS who reported to the President through the Secretary of Defense, he really only had command authority for the Army forces included. Command authority over the personnel assigned from the other branches remained with their respective services.

"I was the Joint Task Force Commander with no overall command authority," said Vaught. "It takes two things to have command authority: the ability to write efficiency reports and the legal authority to Court Martial. I only had those with respect to the Army personnel assigned to the task force."

Vaught's first task was to determine what forces would be needed for the task force. Another problem was there was no specific funding for the JTF and its mission. It would be entirely dependent on funding from the services providing personnel. This is an extremely touchy situation because no command in any of the services likes to give up operational control over any of its forces, much less provide funding for forces it cannot use to support its individual missions.

"We literally had to beg, borrow, and steal personnel, funds, equipment, and support facilities throughout the entire planning and training process," said Vaught.

Air Force Colonel Jim Kyle had been designated Vaught's deputy commander for planning, training, rehearsing, and directing the JTF in conducting a rescue mission. Kyle was selected for the job by Air Force General Bob Taylor who was running a crisis action group at the National Military Command Center associated with the Iran hostage situation. Taylor chose Kyle because of his approximately ten years of experience in special operations, especially with the Air Force C-130 aircraft and its various derivations in support of missions in Vietnam and elsewhere. Kyle had logged 6,000 flying hours in the C-130 including 1,000 of those hours in combat in Vietnam. Vaught assigned Kyle to take immediate control of the Air Force component of the mission with the rest of the deputy commander duties to be sorted out once the task force was more fully manned.

"Jim Kyle was a good officer and a good man," said Vaught. "He was very smart and was a great asset to the mission."

Later, Air Force Major General Philip Gast was added to the task force as a deputy commander. Gast had been at the U.S. Embassy in Tehran until just before the hostage crisis began. He was extremely familiar with the Iranian military capabilities and also the political situation within Iran.

General Jones met each morning with key task force members including Vaught and Kyle. On the first morning after Vaught's initial briefing, Jones set forth the parameters the task force would operate under. He immediately stressed that no one outside the task force team would be allowed to know what the team was doing. Special telephones and teletype machines were installed for security reasons, and working papers had to be tightly guarded and given to the security section for destruction when no longer needed.

Jones stressed that President Carter would have to give final approval to whatever plan was ultimately developed. He also said the State Department had to be kept out of the planning loop because of its opposition to any military option. Jones described the final mission as a "surgical operation" that would include clandestine insertion of the forces into Tehran, a surprise entry into the embassy and freeing of the hostages, and a rapid exfiltration of the rescue force and hostages with "as little violence and loss of life on either side as possible."

Jones also nixed any contact with other existing special operations personnel in other commands or with any of the foreign special operations units such as the SAS, GSG-9, or Israeli commandos. The Chairman limited jumping off points for the mission to Diego Garcia and Egypt, eliminating possible options in Oman, Saudi Arabia, Turkey, Israel, Kuwait, Pakistan, Bahrain, Qatar, and the United Arab Emirates for security reasons. The Chairman questioned Rear Admiral "Dutch" Schoultz, liaison for the Chief of Naval Operations, about the possibility of some type of helicopter launch from a ship operating in the Indian Ocean. Schoultz said such a launch might be possible, but he wasn't particularly interested in using an aircraft carrier as the launch platform because it would disrupt normal fighter operations.

Finally, the question of intelligence was addressed with help requested from the CIA, Defense Intelligence Agency, FBI, National Security Agency, Defense Communications Agency, and the Defense Mapping Agency. Jones promised to get all of the Department of Defense intelligence assets moving to support the task force. The CIA was another matter because requests for help from that agency by the task force for intelligence information about what was going on in Iran had been not met with much cooperation so far. At the beginning, the best source of information about what was happening in Tehran was through nightly news broadcasts by Iranian television.

"Intelligence information is a key to success for any mission, something that is often missed by many commanders, but we weren't going to launch any mission until we had a way to get into and out of the embassy without a massacre occurring in the streets," said Vaught.

In the days that followed the first briefings, task force members tapped every available source of information they could. Because the United States had been the major military supplier to Iran during the Shah's reign, there was considerable information available, especially about Iran's air force and air defense systems capabilities. Former military advisers to Iran were interviewed. It was determined where the weak points in the air defense radar systems were located—that night operation capabilities by the air force were minimal and that anti-aircraft guns were not a threat. A night insertion of the forces into Iran without detection or resistance was deemed highly probable.

The first break for the task force came on November 20 when thirteen hostages were released and sent back to the United States. The released hostages were all debriefed when they got home, providing important information about the interior layout of the embassy, details about the students holding the embassy, their routines, and who the leaders appeared to be.

A model of the embassy compound, all twenty-seven acres and fourteen buildings, was created for Delta, which was now training at Camp Smokey in the North Carolina mountains. The model would be used to study and plan the embassy facilities so that embassy assault tactics could be practiced at Camp Smokey including determination of what weapons would serve Delta best on the mission.

Beckwith argued for all seventy of Delta's current personnel to be included in the mission. Vaught believed anything over forty would be too many. Beckwith outlined the mission and each man's job and won his point for seventy shooters on the mission. It was determined that four helicopters would be needed to transport this size force with two more helicopters for equipment. Later, Beckwith added twenty more men to the Delta contingent increasing the number of helicopters needed to eight.

The Navy determined that an aircraft carrier would be the best launch platform for the helicopters, and Jones confirmed the Navy RH-53D—a long range, heavy lift, ship borne helicopter normal to Navy operations—as the helicopter transport to get Delta to the Tehran area. The RH-53D was currently the only helicopter in the military with in-flight refueling capability. Early on in the planning, in-flight refueling of the helicopters was an option being looked at. In addition, the use of the RH-53D from a carrier allowed for mission security because the helicopters would conduct minesweeping practice in the Indian Ocean, which fit in with the overall Navy profile and would not raise any red flags for the Russians as to why they were aboard the carrier.

The helicopters came from a minesweeping unit stationed at Norfolk, Virginia that had just returned from extensive NATO North operations in Canada. The skipper of the unit, Commander Van Goodloe was alerted to prepare for a secret mission without any further information. Goodloe assumed it was some type of minesweeping countermeasure mission and used that assumption to choose the helicopter crews. Seven five-man crews were initially chosen. On November 20th, Jones ordered Admiral Harry Train, Commander in Chief of the Atlantic, to prepare six RH-53D helicopters for shipment to Diego Garcia from where they would join the aircraft carrier *USS Kitty Hawk*, now patrolling in the Indian Ocean.

The C-130, capable of take-offs and landings on unprepared runways, was chosen as the troop and cargo transport aircraft to get Delta into Iran to a location where they would be joined by the helicopters for the final leg of the insertion. Air Force personnel provided the crews for the C-130s. The DIA was studying aerial photos of the Iranian desert to determine a sight for landing the C-130s and refueling the helicopters for the final leg of the insertion mission.

The AC-130 Spectre gunship, also manned by Air Force personnel, was chosen as the aircraft to provide close air support for Delta on the embassy assault and to potentially conduct strikes on other military targets in the Tehran area, if necessary, to help Delta and the hostages withdraw from the embassy grounds.

Because of the distances involved from jumping off points to Tehran, a two-night mission was decided upon with the helicopters and C-130s flying separately to a desert location where refueling would take place on the helicopters. The helicopters would then transport Delta to a location outside of Tehran where it would hole up during the daylight hours of the next day. After night fall, Delta would be transported by truck to the Embassy to rescue the hostages and extract them from the Embassy grounds. After the hostage rescue on the second night, Delta and the hostages would proceed to an extraction airfield near Tehran where they would be flown out of Iran to safety. Army Rangers would be used to secure both the desert insertion airfield and extraction airfield outside of Tehran.

It was initially decided the helicopters would be manned with Navy pilots and crew chiefs with the Marine co-pilots and door gunners. Navy Captain Jerry Hatcher, from the CNO staff would obtain the helicopters and spare parts for the mission and set up a training program for the pilots. Marine Colonel "Chuck" Pittman, a member of the JCS staff and considered one of the foremost helicopter experts in the Marine Corps, would assist Hatcher and advise Jones and Vaught on the helicopter component of the task force.

Slightly more than two weeks after Vaught had assumed command of the task force, many of the initial problems in planning had been solved. Now dubbed "Operation Rice Bowl," the plan called for a two-night mission where various units involved would launch from widely diverse geographical areas and meet up at a desert location in Iran for refueling before proceeding to the layover location near Tehran. The second night would involve freeing the hostages and moving Delta and the hostages to an airport near Tehran where they would be loaded for transport out of Iran.

The command and control needed to get all the JTF assets into position at the proper time from their various jumping off points was complex. The planning group, headed by Vaught and Kyle, would also direct training and supervise rehearsals as well as take part in the actual mission. Each commander of the respective units involved would conduct the initial training of his forces so they would be ready to participate in combined JTF rehearsals later and would lead his forces through the entire mission.

The unit training would be conducted at their respective bases throughout the United States and at overseas locations in the Pacific for two of the Air Force components. Mission training would be conducted in addition to the normal unit activities at the various bases in order to maintain operational security. Maintaining the outward appearance of normal activities was considered necessary in order to keep the various intelligence assets of the Soviet Union in the dark about anything special going on.

"We were sure that the Russians would tip off the Iranians that a rescue attempt was being prepared for if they saw any unusual activity," said Vaught. "Their spy satellites and other intelligence assets kept track of all our military operations just as we did theirs, so we had to be constantly aware of not making anything look unusual to their intelligence analysts."

Vaught selected Kyle to act as the JTF air component commander and to direct the training program for the Air Force units. Vaught would visit all the units at their home training stations in the United States to monitor training and make sure they were each developing the required levels of proficiency to support the overall plan. Vaught had directed that all rescue operations in Iran would be conducted without lights, so the helicopters and C-130s would perform flight training operations under blacked-out conditions and would concentrate on developing night vision goggle tactics.

As individual unit training got under way, the helicopter crews joined Delta at Camp Smokey for a short time before being moved to the Yuma (AZ) Army Air Station. Almost immediately, problems arose. The pilots had no experience with special operations or night, low-level flying experience. Additionally, Navy regulations forbid night training under blacked-out conditions. The entire operation they were being asked to perform was totally unfamiliar to them.

December 4th was set as the first joint training exercise. The Night-One scenario would be tested at the Yuma Proving Ground Range to determine where more concentrated effort was needed in training. At this point, the plan called for Delta to ride aboard the helicopters from the aircraft carriers to the desert refueling site.

The exercise was run through on two consecutive nights, and both times the helicopter pilots struggled with night vision, low-level flying conditions with the added distraction of dust from the desert floor. Several of the pilots nearly lost control of their aircraft as they were trying to land. After two nights of this, Beckwith didn't want his troops flying with the pilots any longer and Vaught, in an impromptu meeting after the second night, said something had to be done about the helicopter operation very soon. Gast and Pittman agreed that most of the helicopter crews, including Commander Goodloe, had to be replaced. Vaught accepted their recommendation and told them to quickly bring in the best people available.

Nine of the Navy pilots, including Goodloe, were replaced with Marine pilots. Hatcher left with the Navy pilots, leaving Pittman in sole coordination of helicopter operations. The new flight commander was Lieutenant Colonel Ed Seiffert, a Marine Vietnam veteran with considerable helicopter flying experience in the Marine CH-53 helicopter, a similar craft to the RH-53D. Seiffert arrived on December 9th and helped select the remaining Marine pilots who would now perform the mission. Goodloe was sent to Kitty Hawk to oversee the maintenance and flight preparation of the helicopters that would be used in the actual mission.

A second rehearsal was scheduled for December 18th and 19th with Night-One operations tested the first night and Night-Two operations on the second night. Again, there were some problems with the helicopters, this time with the Blade Inspection Method (BIM) warning system. Six helicopters left simulating the flight from the carrier, but only four landed at the simulated refueling site. In the Night-Two exercise, Vaught, who would be at the extraction airfield on the actual mission, was accidentally left behind by the helicopters, a mistake that did not please him one bit.

At the critique after the two-night exercise, Vaught hammered hard at the helicopter force telling them they had to get night flying proficiency up to standard quickly as well as maintenance capabilities. He told them to "make damn sure that six helicopters make it through the entire exercise" the next time a joint exercise was conducted.

A BIM warning means there is a loss of nitrogen pressure in a rotor blade. Rotor blades are basically hollow and are filled with nitrogen gas under pressure. If nitrogen pressure is lost, the BIM warning light comes on. The leak could be caused by anything from a crack in the rotor blade to a faulty filler blade. When a BIM warning light comes on, the manual for the RH-53D calls for the helicopter to land, shut down the engine, and inspect the blades. If a large crack is found, there should be no more flying. However, if a small crack or no crack is found, the manual says the helicopter may continue flying for up to fifteen more hours.

The Marines normally flew CH-53s, which had only a mechanical warning system. IF a BIM warning occurs in this helicopter, Marine doctrine calls for immediate shutdown of the helicopter with no more flying until the problem is fixed. This differed from the Navy doctrine because of the difference in the warning systems in the two helicopter types. All of the experience of the Marine pilots was that a BIM warning meant immediate shutdown. This would play a big role during the actual mission.

Vaught also felt the mission helicopters were not given top priority by the Navy. Thirty RH-53Ds had been purchased when Admiral James Holloway was CNO from 1974-78. The best of these went to Atlantic Fleet operations because the Atlantic Fleet was the one most concerned with potential operations against the Soviet navy in the event of war. Approximately 400 spare blades had been purchased with the best 200 going to the Atlantic Fleet, another 100 to the Pacific Fleet, and the final 100, those deemed to be the most inferior, held in reserve. It was from the 100 reserve blades that the mission helicopters were maintained.

"All along I felt there was a built-in likelihood of failure with the helicopters because we got the sorriest equipment the Navy had available," Vaught said. "It was my opinion the Navy didn't believe the rescue mission would go forward and the equipment for the task force was treated as an afterthought."

Shortly after beginning training, Seiffert decided that nine of his pilots needed to be replaced. Kyle came up with the idea of getting veteran Air Force special operations helicopter pilots included in the new group. They were familiar with this type of flying and could get up to speed on the type of helicopters being used in a short time. He took the idea to General Taylor who agreed to take it to General Jones.

When Kyle spoke with General Taylor later that day, he was told that all Marine replacements had been picked for the helicopter force. The decision was final, and the replacements had already been picked and were on their way to Yuma.

Kyle later learned from an assistant on the Chairman's staff that Jones was embroiled with Marine Corps staff in the Pentagon about the possibility of Marine fighters coming under the command of a joint service theater air commander in wartime. This was a theoretical argument, but one that demonstrates the inter-service jealousies that occur during Pentagon planning. Jones reportedly decided he could not take the helicopter mission for the hostage rescue away from the Marines while the Marine fighter argument was ongoing. It was a decision that would come back to haunt the task force and the mission.

Major General Vaught with Colonel Charles Beckwith in 1980

Chapter Sixteen

Shortly after the second December exercise, word came down from Chairman Jones ordering a two-week break over Christmas and New Year's with work on the mission resuming January 2nd. The reported reason for this stand-down was that the task force units had been in training since early November with no break. It was also felt that not allowing the troops to be with their families over the normal Christmas holidays may make the Soviets take notice of continuing training and may raise security concerns.

Vaught felt that the Chairman was being obstructive, at times making things difficult for him, but he passed along the order. What is puzzling is that the task force had been training and operating under a "be ready to go in ten days" stance. Now it was being ordered to go home for longer than that. This was just another example of the seemingly on again, off again attitude toward the mission of the Chairman and other Pentagon chiefs.

During this break, Vaught went to his boss, General Otis, to address the possibility of relieving Beckwith from his position as Delta commander. Vaught and Beckwith didn't like each other. Vaught felt that Beckwith had operated as a loose cannon, answerable to virtually no one, when he was a SOG commander in Vietnam and that he had carried this attitude with him ever since.

"Charlie was not a team player and not capable of being one," said Vaught. "He wanted Delta to be the focus of the mission, dictating what the other units could and could not do, instead of acting as the unit commander of just one component of the overall rescue mission."

Ultimately it was decided to leave Beckwith in place because of possible morale problems within Delta if he was replaced.

"About one-half of the Delta troopers were completely loyal to Beckwith," said Vaught. "These were basically the old line SOG operators who Charlie had first recruited for Delta and who became the nucleus of Delta at the beginning. They were very competent, highly skilled operators, especially on aircraft hostage recovery – an early and continuing mission of Delta."

However, Beckwith's continuing concerns/criticisms of the helicopters would plague the mission preparations continuously and, ultimately, cause the mission to abort. Understanding Beckwith's fear of the Jolly Green Giant heavy helicopters probably goes back to his Vietnam experiences while leading Hungs and other irregulars through the jungles of central Vietnam. Depending on helicopters for supplies and support, the Jolly Green Giants either didn't show at all or, if they did, it was too little too late. Because of this, many of Beckwith's best native fighters went hungry and at times had to be left behind, an aircraft commander decision.

In one incident, Beckwith had been ordered to return to headquarters on a helicopter when he wanted to stay with his commandos. Considering his past experiences, one could understand why Beckwith did not trust the mission helicopters and pilots.

The return of the various units after the Christmas break brought continued planning and renewed training. With the increased number of helicopters, due to the increase in the number of Delta troopers now included in the mission, the concept of air dropping fuel bladders for refueling the helicopters on Night One of the mission was dropped in favor of loading two 3,000-gallon bulk bladders on board a C-130 aircraft complete with pumps, filters, and hoses. With this configuration, three C-130s could refuel up to ten helicopters, if necessary, on night one before the helicopters continued to Tehran.

The mission helicopters themselves were transferred from the *USS Kitty Hawk* to the *USS Nimitz*, which had arrived on station in the Indian Ocean to relieve the *Kitty Hawk*. Along the way, the *Nimitz* had picked up two additional RH-53D helicopters bringing the total available for the mission on board to eight. However, none of these was in particularly good shape. The helicopters aboard the *Kitty Hawk* had basically been kept below decks with very limited flying time. In addition, spare parts were very limited and maintenance checklists had been ignored. Squadron Commander Van Goodloe and the Navy pilots who had been replaced early in the desert night training had been sent by the Navy to perform on-board maintenance and to be sure they were on the mission helicopters on the carrier. He was not having much success because the Navy supply and maintenance system for the helicopters was inadequate and always a low priority.

The Task Force put together a solid joint exercise at the end of January at desert locations in Nevada. Night One of the mission included securing an airfield with Army Rangers, flying in the C130s and helicopters, refueling the helicopters and transferring Delta to them, and withdrawing the C-130s all under blacked-out operation conditions. Night Two consisted of surveillance and takedown of the embassy, coordination and live fire demonstration of the AC-130 gunships with the ground forces, and exfiltration and withdrawal of all forces when and where needed. All who saw the AC-130 demonstration were impressed.

The success of the two-night exercise proved the plan was workable and the forces were well-prepared to carry it out. General Vaught reported to General Jones and his staff that a workable plan existed, but he came away from the meeting disappointed.

"There had supposedly been some movement in the diplomatic end to get the hostages released, so we were on the back burner again," said Vaught. "I never really believed that the Chairman, the Navy, or the CIA believed we would ever get presidential approval to attempt a rescue of the hostages."

There was also considerable criticism of the mission planning going on behind closed doors. According to the Pentagon grapevine, the task force was relying too much on bold initiative with insufficient forces. The "geniuses" in the Pentagon had concluded that the task force lacked overwhelming force and firepower, according to the Principles of War. In Vaught's view, those "geniuses" had obviously forgotten that this was not supposed to be an invasion of Iran. Instead it was supposed to be a small force, secret mission to snatch the hostages away from their captors and get away with a minimum loss of life on both sides.

In February, Pittman and RH-53 maintenance specialist Captain Larry Sherwood made a trip to the *Nimitz* to check on the status and maintenance progress with the helicopters. They found there was almost none. Six of the helos had been flown only a few hours in the past two and one-half months while the final two had been cannibalized to provide spare parts for the others. The word had not gotten to the *Nimitz* that eight helicopters would be needed for the mission instead of the originally planned six. The admiral commanding the carrier task force had apparently ordered the helicopters be preserved to support future clearing and planting mine operations. The admiral, who had spent time with the task force before he took command of the *Nimitz*, had obviously not been told that the mining operations were nothing but a cover story for having the helos on board the carrier.

Pittman worked out a flying schedule with the commanding officer of the *Nimitz* and the admiral to ensure the helos would get 25-30 hours per month of flight time with sorties of the same approximate duration as would be required by the mission. Sherwood worked out a set of maintenance procedures and requirements with the maintenance crews aboard the carrier. It was also agreed that the Special Operations Division and Navy Headquarters in Washington would receive daily reports on the maintenance status and flying time of the helicopters.

Back in December, Vaught had established a monthly briefing of the Joint Chiefs in the "tank," a secure briefing room on the second floor of the Pentagon used by the Joint Chiefs. During the February briefing, Vaught told the chiefs that by the end of March, the task force would have an emergency capability for rescuing the hostages, but by the end of April the mission would have a "high likelihood of success."

March saw hopes for a diplomatic solution to the hostage crisis dim and increased cooperation from such agencies as the CIA. The task force continued to work on improving the operational components of the plan, but the helicopters remained a worrisome problem.

Early in the month, Vaught, a general who believed in a hands-on approach, requested permission to visit the *Nimitz* to check on the readiness of the helicopters since the helos were the only part of the force that he had not personally scrutinized at this point.

"A three-star Marine [Director of J-3 of the Joint Staff] denied my request," Vaught said. "The J-3 made up some excuse about not being able to provide a convincing cover story for my presence on the carrier. However, I really believe they were trying to hide the fact that the helos were still in bad shape."

The two helicopters that had been added to the mission still had not been in the air because of a shortage of critical parts. The Navy was not living up to the promises it had made earlier, and Vaught wanted to know why. The maintenance and flight operations of the helicopters were the total responsibility of the Navy, and Vaught was upset by the reports he was receiving.

In February, while Vaught was presenting a briefing to the Joint Chiefs about the plan and readiness of the Joint Task Force, he was asked by Admiral Thomas Hayward, Chief of Naval Operations, what his major concern was in being totally ready to conduct the rescue mission.

"Your helicopters aboard the Nimitz, Admiral," Vaught replied.

Vaught then expounded on his frustrations with the maintenance status of the mission's helicopters and the fact that he had been denied the opportunity to visit the carrier to observe firsthand the maintenance and readiness of the helicopters. Hayward denied any knowledge of the refusal for Vaught to visit the carrier.

Meanwhile in Iran, the CIA had an agent reporting back on the location of the hostages and conditions around the embassy. However, the task force wanted its own man on the ground to conduct intelligence for the mission. Dick Meadows was a retired, 30-year Army special operations operative who had risen to legendary status during the Vietnam War. He had acted as a civilian adviser to Delta Force during its startup and was called back to go into Iran.

Meadows flew to Tehran under the name of "Richard Keith" with an Irish passport and a cover story. He successfully passed through Iranian immigration with no problems. Meadows performed surveillance on the American embassy and also did reconnaissance on Delta's planned route into Tehran from its Day Two hiding place outside the city.

"Meadows called in twice a week with updated intelligence," Vaught said. "Meadows was able to obtain a key to the stadium across the street from the embassy that we were going to use as a collection point for the extraction. His team was also able to determine the type and conditions of the weapons being used by the students holding the hostages."

The last day of March saw John Carney perform a night-time reconnaissance on the proposed Desert One site that would serve as the staging area inside Iran on Night One before Delta moved on to its hiding place outside Tehran. Carney was checking the desert floor for aviation operations as well as laying out landing lights for the temporary airstrip. Two days later, Masirah Island off the coast of Oman was approved as a staging base for the C-130s and Delta at the beginning of the mission. This both made the trip shorter for Delta and eliminated the need for it to ride the helicopters all the way from the carrier to Tehran. The good news was piling onto the task force at this point.

April 13th was the day the operation became reality. President Carter, frustrated by being jerked around in his diplomatic attempts, decided to go forward with the rescue mission. On the same day, Vaught had called a meeting of all Joint Task Force commanders and supporting staff at Fort Bragg, North Carolina to review the entire rescue plan thoroughly and make sure each leader clearly understood the role of his personnel in the rescue scenario. After each commander presented the details of his part of the mission, the group went to lunch and reconvened to face a murder board. Vaught had first used a murder board in late February to conduct "what-if" drills on every segment of the mission. Now, it would test the planning for Desert One, which had become the Night One meeting place only recently.

"Murder boards are not popular, but I think they have a place in planning missions such as this one," Vaught said. "The concept was to make sure the plans and procedures we had developed were sound and to determine what alternative options were available if things did not go according to plan, which they rarely do."

The task force had performed five major rehearsals of the mission during training using USMC West Coast-based helos. Vaught was of the opinion that the mission had a very good chance of succeeding despite the problems with the helicopters on board the *Nimitz*.

"I knew the Sikorski helicopters on the *Nimitz* were shit, but would fly," he said. "They were over hours for routine maintenance and not in prime shape. The helicopters were the Achilles heel of the whole operation from the beginning, but, in spite of all the difficulties with them, I still believed we had an improving capability to do what we set out to do in November 1979."

As it looked that the mission would go forward, Vaught got an extremely unusual request from JCS Chairman Jones.

"He told me to put together a comprehensive failure plan," said Vaught. "I said I had never heard that term before and asked what it consisted of."

Jones told Vaught to go through every phase of the mission and identify the number of helicopters that would be needed to continue. The failure plan called for six helicopters to be mission capable at Desert One for the rescue attempt to go forward.

"That was the stupidest request I had ever heard in my whole career," Vaught said. "My combat experience confirmed if you give somebody an excuse not to do what the mission calls for, they have an opportunity to quit at their election. About one-half of the people will quit when they have to contend with what appears to be a high-risk mission block. My policy has always been to press on, and your best subordinates will find a way to succeed. Failure is not an option in my book."

On the evening of April 13th, Vaught, Jones, Gast, and Beckwith went to the White House to brief President Carter on the mission.

"We went through every part of the mission with the President," said Vaught. "The President said he would not interfere with operational decisions during the mission and gave us the tentative go ahead for April 25th."

Vaught said the President warned against "wanton killings," but he agreed the rescue force was authorized to use whatever force was necessary to protect American lives. The President also asked about the anticipated number of casualties and was told between three and eight casualties were estimated including both hostages and rescue personnel.

The final mission plan, code-named "Eagle Claw," called for three troop-carrying MC-130s and three fuel-bearing EC-130s to leave Masirah and fly to Desert One. The MC-130s would transport the ninety-three Delta troops plus twenty-five other support troops that included six truck drivers, six translators, and the thirteen Rangers that would take down the Foreign Ministry building.

"The front seat of the trucks would have one native Iranian driver, one Farsi speaking U.S. serviceman, and one Delta troop carrying an AK-47 in case of trouble," said Vaught. "In case of trouble I wanted a native Iranian driving because, when the cold steel of a pistol is put against your head, you will speak in your native language."

Launching from the *Nimitz*, the eight helicopters would fly to Desert One, arriving approximately thirty minutes after the 130s. The helicopters would be refueled, load Delta and the support troops, and fly approximately three more hours to a location outside Tehran where Delta would be met by Meadows and his agents, who would lead Delta to a remote location sixty-five miles outside Tehran where they would spend the daylight hours of Day Two. After off-loading Delta, the helicopters would fly another fifteen minutes to their hide sight for Day Two.

After dark on Day Two, two of the DOD agents would return to Delta's location with a Datsun pickup truck and a Volkswagen bus. The bus would take the drivers and translators to a location outside Tehran to pick up six Mercedes trucks while the pickup truck would take Beckwith on a reconnaissance of the route to the embassy. After Beckwith checked the area around the embassy, he would return to the hide sight where the trucks would already be waiting.

Delta—split up into Red, White, and Blue Elements—would board the trucks at approximately 8:30 p.m. for the drive to the embassy. The 13-man Ranger contingent would go to the Foreign Ministry by separate route in the Volkswagen bus. Between 11 p.m. and midnight, the assault would start with a select group of Delta operators driving up to the embassy in the Datsun pickup, taking down the two guard posts and any walking guards on Roosevelt Avenue (the street alongside the embassy complex). Red,

White, and Blue, following a short distance behind, would go to a spot on Roosevelt Avenue, across from the soccer stadium, and climb over the embassy walls.

The Red Element, consisting of forty men, would secure the western end of the complex, releasing any hostages found in the commissary or staff cottages as well as neutralizing any guards in the motor pool and power plant areas. The Blue Element, another 40-man unit, would secure the eastern end of the complex, releasing hostages in the Ambassador and Deputy Chief of Mission residences and the chancellery. The White Element, a 13-man group, was responsible for securing and covering of Roosevelt Avenue, with machine guns set up at each end, for the eventual transfer of the hostages and Delta from the embassy complex to the soccer stadium.

Inside the compound, once the Red Element (which had the farthest distance to travel) was in place, the wall surrounding the embassy compound would be blown, signaling the beginning of the assault on the buildings. The hole in the wall would provide a quick withdrawal route from the embassy to the soccer stadium across the street, which would be the assembling area for the hostages and Delta.

The helicopters would pick up the hostages and Delta troopers and transfer them thirty-five miles to an unused airport at Manzariyeh, which would be secured by another Ranger force that was flown in on the second night. Once everyone was at Manzariyeh—hostages, drivers, translators, helicopter pilots and crews, DOD agents, Rangers, and Delta—they would all board C-141 Starlifters for the flight to freedom.

Contingency plans were set in case there were not enough helicopters remaining to evacuate everyone to Manzariyeh in one trip, an effort that would use three helicopters from the soccer stadium and another from the Foreign Ministry. In such a case, Delta would set up a defensive perimeter around the soccer stadium while the remaining helicopters completed the evacuation in shuttle runs. In the unlikely event that no helicopter could return to the soccer stadium for Delta, it was prepared to evade and escape overland.

The mission was approved, and it was now onward to Iran. April 25th was set as the day of the insertion of the rescue forces. A 12-day lead time to mission launch was required to move the thirty-four mission and twenty support aircraft plus hundreds of mission and support personnel approximately 8,000 miles to the staging bases without detection by the Soviet military electronic intelligence and humint assets around the world.

CH-53 Helicopters aboard the *USS Nimitz* in April 1980

Chapter Seventeen

After President Carter approved the deployment of the Joint Task Force, the job of surreptitiously moving the units from Japan and the United States to locations in the Indian Ocean, Arabian Gulf, and Middle East required skillful use of cover and deception. Detection by Russian spy satellites and signals intelligence sites had to be avoided, and our allies could not be let in on what was happening.

Thirty-four mission aircraft as well as twenty support aircraft and the land units had to be moved 8,000 miles without attracting attention. These were mixed in with a number of flight operations routed through Wadi Kena, Egypt, the mission's forwarding operating base, so as to make the air operations seem routine to observers. These operations began twelve days prior to the April 25th mission start date and were controlled from a master operations chart overseen by Colonel Kyle.

Four days prior to the start of the mission, Vaught and his senior staff arrived at Wadi Kena. They assembled at the large hangar building that would serve as the JTF command center. Across the Indian Ocean, the last of the MC-130s moved to Masirah Island, the forward staging base for Night One. The AC-130 gunships and Delta left the next day to make the trip to Egypt.

While the transfer of planes, troops, and equipment was taking place, Dick Meadows was inside Iran with several other Department of Defense agents checking out the hiding places for the assault forces and observing and reconnoitering the embassy compound and the route Delta would take into the city. Meadows also visited the soccer stadium across from the embassy posing as a European soccer agent looking to book a soccer match. During this visit, Meadows gathered some key intelligence that would be needed to conduct the helicopter transfer of hostages and Delta troopers from the embassy to the stadium for extraction.

On April 23rd, word reached the command center that updated intelligence located fifty of the hostages together in the embassy's chancellery building. Up until that information, the hostages were believed to have been held in several different locations in the embassy complex, causing Delta planning to include the storming and clearing of several buildings in the complex. This information actually reduced the number of Delta troopers that would have been needed for the assault because only one building would be involved in the embassy complex. However, it was decided not to reduce the size of the assault force in case the information proved to be faulty and a shift to the other buildings was needed. Three of the hostages continued to be held in the Iranian Foreign Ministry building.

A plan revision now called for the Red Element to concentrate its entire effort on taking down and freeing the hostages in the chancellery building with eight troopers from Blue added to its force. The reduced Blue Element would now neutralize the guards in the motor pool and power plant areas and concentrate on security inside the embassy compound.

The helicopter pilots reached the *Nimitz* on April 20th along with several key spare parts needed to get two of the helicopters more mission ready. The last helicopter included in the mission had not been flown since arriving on the *Nimitz* nearly 100 days earlier because of an ongoing replacement of the rotor transmission assembly. With the help of Sikorsky technical representatives, this work was completed and the "hangar queen" reached operational status for the mission.

However, Vaught was apprised of an even bigger problem with the helicopters. Pittman advised Vaught that some of the secure radio systems on the helicopters did not work, and there were no spare parts to fix them. Vaught reluctantly gave permission to remove the secure portions of the UHF and FM radios on board the helicopters. This meant the helicopter crews would have to communicate between aircraft by lights and hand signals while in the air or break radio silence with non-secure (plain language) transmissions in urgent circumstances.

Delta held an impromptu religious service on April 24th, at the start of which Vaught addressed the troops including a passage from Scripture. "In the book of Isaiah, the Scripture says, 'And I heard the voice of the Lord saying, "Whom shall I send, and who will go for us?" And Isaiah said, "Here am I! Send me."' Men, your country is counting on you. You've stepped forward and said, 'Here am I, Lord. Send me!' God bless you."

Captain Jerry Boykin of Delta, a man of deep religious faith who would go on to become a Lieutenant General and command the U.S. Army Special Operations Command before he retired in September 2007, conducted the short service.

Boykin began by saying, "You know, about three thousand years ago, right in this very desert where we're standing, God led the Israelites out of bondage. They traveled across this same desert to a new freedom. And I believe God has called us to lead fifty-three Americans out of bondage and back to freedom." Boykin followed with a prayer, and all of Delta sang 'God Bless America.' Then, they moved to board the C-141s for the flight to Masirah Island from which it would move to Desert One the next night.

As the Delta troopers stood in line waiting to be checked off on the loading manifest, Vaught mingled among them shaking hands, telling anecdotes to try and calm tight nerves. He spoke with every man who deployed that day.

Delta landed at Masirah at approximately 1400 hours (2 p.m.). Soft drinks, water, and lots of ice had been set out for the men, and tents had been put up to provide some protection from the sun. Most of the troops got off their feet in the tents. Four hours later, Delta was in the air aboard the MC-130s on its way to Desert One. Most of the troops slept along the way, according to Beckwith's account.

At 2200 hours the first MC-130 landed at Desert One, and the Road Watch Team, composed of Rangers and Delta support troops, moved to quickly set up roadblocks to guard the site's flanks. Before they could reach position, a black Mercedes bus, filled with Iranian civilians, was stopped with the Iranians being herded off the side of the road under guard. Shortly thereafter, two small trucks came down the dirt road intersecting Desert One. The lead truck was stopped with an anti-tank weapon and set on fire. The driver of that truck ran to the second truck, which reversed and escaped; however, it was decided that the occupants of the trucks were probably smugglers, probably hadn't seen much, and wouldn't report anything. The helicopters were due in thirty minutes as Delta broke into three groups to pre-position for loading.

While the C-130 operation went smoothly, the helicopter operation did not. Approximately 145 miles into Iran, Helicopter 6 developed a BIM warning. The Marine pilots immediately landed and confirmed the BIM warning. Marine helicopter doctrine on a BIM warning directs the helicopter to be grounded until the problem is repaired. The Navy, which utilizes two BIM warnings, allows for another eighteen hours of flying with one BIM warning, but, although these were Navy helicopters, they were being flown by Marine pilots. Helicopter 6 was abandoned as Helicopter 8 landed nearby and picked up the flight crew.

Approximately forty-five minutes later, the helicopters encountered their first haboob, a desert condition where the sand rises from the desert floor in a dense, cloud-like dust formation. They successfully passed through the first haboob, but, shortly thereafter, they encountered a second haboob. This is where the potential mission-stopping problems really began.

Seiffert, the flight leader in Helicopter 1, lost sight of the ground and most of his helicopters. He decided to reverse course, land, and determine the next move. Helicopter 2, the only other one that could see Seiffert, followed. As Helicopters 1 and 2 made a 180-degree turn, exited the haboob, and landed, Helicopters 3, 4, 5, 7, and 8 continued onward toward Desert One. Seiffert received word that the MC-130s were landing at Desert One and decided to get back on track to the site. He and Helicopter 2 again entered the second haboob bound for Desert One.

Helicopter 5 began experiencing flight instrument problems, started falling behind, and eventually lost sight of the rest of the formation. Approximately fifty miles from getting out of the second haboob and 150 miles from Desert One, the pilot of Helicopter 5 decided to turn around and head back to the *Nimitz*. The co-pilot of Helicopter 5 reportedly disagreed with turning around and urged his pilot to go on because "this was the Super Bowl," but he was overruled.

Meanwhile, Helicopter 2 lost its second-stage hydraulic pump, which powers the No. 1 Automatic Flight Control System and the backup of the primary flight controls. Peacetime flying rules call for a "land as soon as possible" action with this type of malfunction. The pilot suspected a leak in the hydraulic system and decided to fly on to Desert One in the hopes of repairing the problem there. At this point, Helicopter 6 was out of the mission sitting in the desert while Helicopter 5 was proceeding back to the carrier and Helicopter 2 had hydraulic system problems but was continuing on. This left only the minimum number of six helicopters proceeding to Desert One with one of those having mechanical problems.

Helicopters 3, 4, and 7 finally arrived at Desert One approximately one hour behind schedule. Helicopter 8 followed approximately twenty minutes later with Helicopters 1 and 2 arriving approximately five minutes later. Although the mission was 1.5 hours behind schedule, six helicopters were preparing to refuel and load Delta for the final leg of the journey to the hide sight outside Tehran.

However, the Marine pilots were shaken up from their experience with the sand haboob. Kyle reports one of the pilots saying to him, "That was the worst sandstorm I've ever flown through. We ought to call this off, leave the helicopters, and get out of here." Kyle told the pilot they had to go on.

Kyle moved on to talk to Seiffert. He arrived just as Beckwith was leaving the lead pilot. Kyle reported Seiffert saying, "It's nice to talk to somebody who's still in control of his faculties and can calmly discuss the situation." Seiffert also reported that flying through the suspended dust had drained the helicopter crews both physically and mentally, but the helicopters would go forward.

At this point, Kyle called Vaught on a satellite phone to confirm the status of the two missing helicopters. Vaught told him they were not enroute to Desert One. Kyle acknowledged that just six helicopters remained for the mission and requested to have KC-135 tankers remain on station as long as possible to refuel the MC-130s on their way back to Masirah. He then told Vaught the helicopters would be back in the air in approximately twenty minutes.

While Kyle was communicating with Vaught, it was discovered the pump for the second-stage hydraulic system on Helicopter 2 was burned out because of a lack of hydraulic fluid. The pilot reported this to Seiffert who directed him to shut the helicopter down and abort the mission. When Kyle joined the discussion, Seiffert confirmed to him that he had grounded Helicopter 2 as unsafe.

According to Kyle, the pilot of Helicopter 2, B.J. McGuire, had presumed the problem was a burned-out pump that could probably not be repaired at Desert One. McGuire's plan was to get the necessary spare part at Desert One, continue on to the hide sight with one working pump, and replace the burned-out pump the next day. Seiffert's order countermanded that plan.

In Kyle's mind, several thoughts were conflicted. He was not a helicopter pilot and would accept Seiffert's decision, but, the mission was being flown under wartime standards where aircraft were expected to fly in degraded mechanical condition in order to complete the mission. Trying to keep the mission from aborting, Kyle asked Seiffert if five helicopters could take Delta and their gear to the hide site. Seiffert replied that the helicopters were at the max and could not carry any more weight.

Kyle next went to Beckwith and asked him if Delta's force could be cut by twenty men (the number carried on one helicopter) and still complete the mission. According to Kyle, Beckwith immediately answered, "No way, I need every man I've got and every piece of gear."

Beckwith confirms this in his book *Delta Force* where he says he told Kyle, "Jim, I can't go forward with five. We gotta go back." (Beckwith meant abandon the mission and go back to Masirah on the C-130s.)

Kyle next called Vaught to inform him that the mission was down to five working helicopters. As he headed for the satellite phone, Delta's men were already getting out of the helicopters and moving toward the MC-130s.

Vaught told Kyle to consult with the other unit leaders (Seiffert and Beckwith) to determine if the mission could go forward with five helicopters. Kyle informed Vaught that discussion had already taken place and both Seiffert and Beckwith insisted they could not cut anything out and continue with five helicopters. Vaught told Kyle to stand by for final instructions.

Beckwith reports in his book that he was immediately angry with Vaught for asking if the mission could go forward with five helicopters because the "Comprehensive Failure Plan" called for at least six helicopters to go forward from Desert One for the mission to continue. He also says he lost all respect for Vaught for even asking the question. Beckwith claims Kyle asked him again and he replied, "Ain't no way Jim. No way! You tell me which of those 130s you want me to load up. Delta's going home."

Vaught called Jones to inform him of the situation at Desert One. Jones called Zbigniew Brzezinski, the President's National Security Adviser, who called Secretary of Defense Harold Brown, who called the President. The President said to go with the decision of the commander in the field. The mission was over.

Thirty years later, the decision to abort still bothers Vaught. "I am totally convinced to this day, if we had gotten to the hide sites, we would have had enough helicopters to finish the mission. We could have gotten by with three at the embassy and one at the Foreign Ministry. I believe the sixth helicopter could have been flown to the hide site with one working pump. The pilot did too. We could have cannibalized one of the helicopters during the next day, if necessary, to make sure we had five in good working order for the rescue."

"Chairman Jones's Comprehensive Failure Plan had killed the mission. In my view, Beckwith never wanted to go to Tehran and Seiffert was too tired to make the right high-risk decision to continue. Hence, the blame for failure to continue the mission belongs primarily to General David Jones," Vaught said. "The mission would have gone smoothly in Tehran. Meadows had done his job and greased the skids. We knew the guards would not give us much trouble as they were basically kids with dirty weapons and limited ammunition."

"If I had been at Desert One, and maybe I should have been, I would have ordered the mission forward. But, I was unwilling to do that from Egypt and left the decision to the on-scene commanders. However, anybody who thinks a military mission in enemy territory is going to go perfectly according to plan and is not prepared to make adjustments as they are called for is only kidding himself. It just doesn't work that way. The stupid 'Comprehensive Failure Plan' provided an excuse to quit, and some chose to use it," Vaught concluded.

There was one more disaster to come at Desert One. As the five remaining helicopters were refueling and preparing to return to the carrier, one of the helicopters mistook a flashlight held by one of the combat controllers standing by an MC-130 as meant to guide him from behind the airplane. The helicopter crashed into the airplane causing an explosion and fire. Eight men died as a result of the incident, but it could have been much worse. All the Delta troopers managed to exit the airplane as it was burning as well as most of the crews from the airplane and the helicopter. It was the incident for which the mission would be best remembered, but one that would not have happened if the mission had not been aborted due to Chairman Jones, who had no life and death combat experience, meddling in high-stress life and death mission plans and decisions.

Major General "Grim Jim" Vaught shortly after the unsuccessful Operation Eagle Claw

Chapter Eighteen

After the disaster in the desert, the various units of the task force made their way back to the United States via Masirah and Wadi Kena. The debriefings, normal at the end of any military mission, took several days. During this time, both the Senate and House Armed Services Committees held closed-door hearings with members of the task force, ostensibly fact-finding hearings, but in reality they were looking to find someone to blame and also to air political differences between Democrats and Republicans with a presidential election coming in November. After a couple weeks of hearings, both Congressional committees decided to drop their investigations.

Two things did come out of the hearings, however. Sen. John Warner, R-VA, appeared to those testifying before the committee to be attempting to find a way to place the blame for the mission's failure on the task force commanders, especially Vaught. Of note here is that Warner was Secretary of the Navy when the RH-53 helicopters, the mission helicopters, were purchased by the Navy. While Warner and his key staff member Robert McFarlane asked such questions as 'were you directed to do something you didn't want to do', they never tried to get to the heart of the matter of why the mission did not move beyond Desert One.

Sen. Henry Jackson, D-WA, questioned why it had taken six months to prepare for the rescue mission. He learned the Joint Task Force inherited the problem of no command structure in place for a joint special operations mission. More importantly, Sen. Sam Nunn, D-GA, asked what could be done to make the system better for the future. This was a subject the joint task force commanders had spoken about for many months. The obvious answer was to establish a new joint command. Beckwith told committee members that a permanent joint service task force should be established with responsibility for counterterrorism missions. This discussion led to the establishment of the Joint Service Special Operations Command.

Vaught had already begun moving in that direction. Upon his return to the United States from Wadi Kena, Vaught was immediately involved in planning for a possible second hostage rescue mission. President Carter had assured Vaught he would have full support for a second mission with anything he wanted in the way of troops and equipment.

"We increased our capabilities," said Vaught. "We put together a menu of possibilities because we didn't have enough intelligence about where the hostages were being held after the Iranians reacted to news of the first mission."

The concept was to develop a force from which several subordinate task forces could be drawn if it was learned that the hostages were being held in several locations throughout the country.

"We wanted the capability to go to between three to five locations around the country and make an effort to simultaneously rescue our people," Vaught said. "We trained to do that while also training to take advantage of increasing mobility."

The staff devised ways to increase range of the helicopters, particularly those in the Army. Satellite communications capability was increasing as was intelligence collection capabilities within the areas of concern of the task force. Vaught said there was a rededication on the part of all the participating elements of the various armed forces to create a thoroughgoing capability to do what might have to be done to make another rescue attempt.

"We went back into the desert, we identified more forces, more mobility and, at one point, we had 10,000 people in the U.S. working on this," Vaught said. "It's a very large joint effort to put together the type of force that needs to be marshalled as a trained, joint, ready-to-go capability."

The staff Vaught put together for the possible second mission essentially became the first Joint Special Operations Command Staff. Major General Richard Scholtes was assigned to the task force in October 1980 as Vaught's replacement. The two worked together until Vaught officially turned over operational command of the task force to Scholtes on December 1, 1980. The Joint Special Operations Command was officially activated on December 15, 1980 with Scholtes serving as its first commander until August 1984.

Vaught returned full-time to his Pentagon position of Director of Operations, Readiness, and Mobilization in the Office of the Deputy Chief of Staff of the Army for Military Operations. He remained there until August 1981 when he was approved for promotion to Lieutenant General and assigned as Commander of the Combined Force Field Army of U.S. and Republic of Korea troops.

While preparations were being made for a possible second rescue effort, Vaught and his unit commanders appeared before the House Armed Services Committee where members were looking for someone to blame for the failure of the mission. After two weeks of investigation, it became clear that there was no one person to blame for the failure to complete the mission. In fact, there was no blame at all from the standpoint of command and control of the task force.

Early in May 1980, the Department of Defense established the Holloway Commission, chaired by recently retired former JCS Chairman Adm. James L. Holloway, III. The commission was made up of six flag officers who were tasked with examining the organization, planning coordination, direction, and control of the Iran hostage rescue mission with a goal to recommend improvements in these areas for the future. Many of the task force members completed appearances before the commission with the impression that the members of the committee would not recognize a special operations mission if one hit them in the face. The general impression was that Adm. Holloway was put in the committee chair to protect the Navy's handling of the helicopters. Holloway was the CNO when the helicopters used in the mission were purchased by the Navy.

During preparations for the mission, Vaught expressed concerns to the Joint Chiefs of Staff that the Navy was not conducting the routine flight operations with the helicopters aboard the carrier that it had been asked to conduct.

"We sent two different groups out to the carrier to see how the helicopters were doing," Vaught said. "Both reported back that they were dissatisfied with the effort being put forth to prepare the helicopters for the mission, and there were a significant number of deficiencies."

"Helicopters aboard a carrier are used for anti-submarine warfare and search and rescue," Vaught said. "They are considered a necessary nuisance, and I expect the ones we had aboard were looked at that way too."

After testifying before the commission, Vaught went to speak to Jones. "I was under the impression that the commission was going to try and blame the failure of the mission on me," Vaught said. "The Navy sabotaged the mission in my opinion. I told Jones that I would keep my mouth shut and not write a book for at least ten years as long as they didn't try to hang fault on me. If they did, I was prepared to immediately resign my commission and hold a press conference on the steps of the Pentagon. I would tell the press exactly who fouled up the mission, and his (Jones) name would be at the top of the list."

Ultimately, the Holloway Commission published a report with eleven major findings, none of which really had anything to do with the mission's failure. It also listed twelve lower priority points the commission considered contributing causes to the mission's failure. Of these, helicopter aborts, selection of alternate helicopter pilots, and helicopter communications actually went to the heart of the mission's failure. The bottom line of the report listed two reasons—helicopter failure rate and low-visibility flying conditions—as factors that combined to cause the mission to abort.

Thirty years later, the reasons for the failure of the mission to go forward from Desert One lead to unpopular conclusions. The Congressional committees, especially Sen. Warner, and the Holloway Commission concentrated on such things as command structures, weather problems, and excessive operational security. They all missed the boat.

The Joint Task Force successfully got the forces and equipment necessary to continue the mission inside Iran without being discovered. The helicopter that was shut down in the desert with the BIM warning could have and should have continued to Desert One. The helicopter that was shut down at Desert One due to hydraulic problems should have been allowed to continue to the hide site outside Tehran. The most puzzling helicopter problem was with the one that flew to within 100 or so miles of Desert One before deciding to turn around and go back to the carrier. This decision was apparently made because of the pilot's reactions to the dust storm problems, but the helicopter had to go back through the areas that had just caused so much trouble on the return trip.

Seiffert's decision to shut down the helicopter with mechanical problems at Desert One and not go forward to the hide site was probably as much of a reaction to the exhaustion the pilots experienced flying through the dust storms. However, the decision to have the five remaining helicopters return to the carrier after refueling, again through the same areas that the dust storms had been located, is difficult to accept. There was only a couple of hours flying time remaining to the hide site rather than the approximately five hours to get back to the carrier.

"I don't know if it should have been Admiral Holloway's group, but some group should have gone to great depths to find out what went wrong with those helicopters," Vaught said. "To say their maintenance was up to standard, if that's the case then their standards are wrong. For heavy helicopters to have significant operational failure indicators after only five hours of flying, we don't need machines like that."

Even without the three helicopters, the mission could have and should have moved forward with five helicopters. However, going back to General Jones and his Comprehensive Failure Plan, anyone who wanted an excuse not to continue the mission had a ready-made excuse to quit, and that is exactly what happened.

"The comprehensive failure plan identified alibis for people and gave them a crutch," Vaught said. "The plan called for a minimum of six helicopters to proceed to Tehran. When we got down to five, they didn't have to consider 'can you go on'. You just automatically quit and come back. The commander on the scene has been relieved from any consideration of continuing the mission because the failure threshold has been identified and met."

Beckwith probably could have cut the Delta contingent by twenty troops and continued on to the hide site near Tehran. Intelligence had already provided information that made the search of the embassy grounds less intensive. All fifty of the hostages Delta was responsible for rescuing were being held in one building, and adjustments had already been made to the Delta teams to provide more perimeter security and less search responsibility within the teams. Beckwith's reaction begs the question – what would he have done if all of Delta got to the hide site, but one of the trucks broke down on the way to the embassy grounds keeping some of the Delta troops from completing the journey? Would he have cancelled the mission at that point because all of Delta's forces were not at the embassy at the start of the actual rescue? Such action would have been pretty difficult to cancel at that point because of the location where it would have occurred. However, when Beckwith was presented with an excuse to quit at Desert One, he took it.

Beckwith's actions are strangely reminiscent of General George B. McClellan in the Civil War. McClellan played a large role in raising, organizing, and training the Army of the Potomac at the beginning of the war into a strong force. However, when he took it out to face General Robert E. Lee and his smaller Army of Northern Virginia in battle, McClellan more often found reasons to avoid fighting rather than taking advantage of the larger size of his force to engage and defeat the Confederates. Beckwith raised, organized, and trained Delta into an exceptional counterterrorism force, but then he failed to engage it in the only actual mission on which he led Delta. Expecting a military operation to go exactly according to plan is unrealistic and should not be used as an excuse to abort mid-operation, but that is exactly what Beckwith did.

The exact opposite approach to Beckwith's in military operations was best demonstrated by General George S. Patton during World War II. Patton concentrated on the final objective, going with what forces he had and adjusting midstream. When the Germans surrounded the 101st Airborne Division at Bastogne during the Battle of the Bulge, Patton moved his 3rd Army 100 miles in forty-eight hours to relieve Bastogne and stop the German counteroffensive. While other American commanders were still discussing the tactical problems at Bastogne, Patton was moving his army to change them.

Vaught speculates that Beckwith was suffering from a form of Post-Traumatic Stress Disorder as a result of his Vietnam experiences. Initially Vaught seriously considered going to Desert One on the first night of the mission to oversee operations there. However, he ultimately decided not to.

"If I was at Desert One, and maybe I should have been, I would have ordered the mission to continue," Vaught said. "I believe to this day we would have successfully gotten the forces and equipment that we needed to the hide site. The second day would have gone very smoothly, and we would have been in and out before the Iranians were totally aware of what happened, in my opinion."

"As the battlefield becomes more and more mechanically and electronically dependent, we're going to have to be very careful about setting the criteria for permitting the machine and its operators to drop out of the campaign with no penalty," Vaught said. "That's sort of where we ended up at Desert One."

The decisions made at Desert One by Beckwith and Seiffert were both questionable at best, especially considering they were within a couple hours of their first night destination and still undetected. However, having the mission fail may have been the preferred option to certain factions back in Washington because it certainly hurt Carter's re-election chances.

Despite being a graduate of the Naval Academy, President Carter was never considered pro-military. During his time in office, Carter opposed military pay raises and reduced the defense budget. Less than two months after the embassy personnel were taken hostage, the Carter administration announced a 28% cut in Navy shipbuilding programs. Nothing gets military service chiefs as hostile as budget cuts in large capital expenditure programs. The Navy admirals were not in favor of Carter's re-election bid.

Joint Task Force planning was always hampered by poor intelligence. CIA Director Stansfield Turner was a retired admiral, actually a classmate of Carter's at the academy. The failure of the Navy to provide adequate maintenance and flight testing to the mission helicopters for most of the first five months of mission planning and preparation was highly questionable, as was the Navy's denial of Vaught's request to visit the carrier and inspect the helicopters. While it can't be definitively stated that the Navy and the CIA actively worked against the success of the mission, it can be said neither entity put forth full efforts to support it.

"All you can do is train and put people through circumstances that approximate the environment that they are expected to encounter in the operation," said Vaught. "You try to judge from that and make adjustments in your plan accordingly and try to underwrite the likelihood of shortfalls and the unexpected exigencies that you will encounter as the operation unfolds."

The lessons learned from Operation Eagle Claw prompted a series of organizational reforms that helped bring about success in later special operations missions. One of the reforms included the creation of Joint Special Operations Command (JSOC) in October 1980. JSOC is the "joint headquarters designed to study special operations requirements and techniques; ensure interoperability and equipment standardization; plan and conduct joint special operations exercises and training; and develop joint special operations tactics," and it was formed after a direct recommendation from Colonel Beckwith. Additionally, it was clear that there was a need for highly-trained Army helicopter pilots who were able to fly low-level night missions, which prompted the creation of the 160th Special Operations Aviation Regiment (SOAR) to serve as a dedicated provider of air support for Special Operations missions. Furthermore, the Special Operations community received its own line of funding called Major Force Program 11 (MFP-11) to help ensure that there would be a budget for these types of missions. Although some of these reforms did not appear until the Goldwater-Nichols Act in 1986, Desert One was a major driving factor for many of the changes.

JOINT SPECIAL OPERATIONS COMMAND

COMMANDER - **U.S. Army Lt. Gen. Austin S. Miller**
SENIOR ENLISTED ADVISOR - **U.S. Army Command Sgt. Maj. Jeffrey W. Wright**

ESTABLISHED - **Oct. 22, 1980**

The JOINT SPECIAL OPERATIONS COMMAND, located at Fort Bragg, North Carolina, is a sub-unified command of the U.S. Special Operations Command. It is charged to study special operations requirements and techniques, ensure interoperability and equipment standardization, plan and conduct Special Operations exercises and training, and develop joint Special Operations tactics.

Joint Special Operations Command

Chapter Nineteen

As Commanding General of the Combined US/ROK Field Army, Vaught was responsible for the defense of approximately 60% of the 150-mile demilitarized zone separating North and South Korea. The units under his command included three corps with six divisions and one brigade in forward deployment and five divisions in reserve along with the U.S. 2nd Infantry Division and the ROK 20th Mechanized Division as field Army reserves. In addition, there were five South Korean ready reserve divisions with their headquarters and equipment located in Vaught's tactical area.

"We were tasked with defending the two most critical corridors the enemy might use to approach Seoul in the event of hostilities," Vaught said. "The corridor in the east, the Chorwon Valley, was the route the North Koreans followed at the initiation of the Korean War in June 1950. The western approach, Route 1, is probably the more dangerous because it's only about thirty miles from the DMZ to the center of Seoul."

At the time Vaught was commanding the combined field army, South Korea had a population of approximately forty million with ten million living in and immediately around Seoul and another ten million within about sixty miles of North Korea.

"My main responsibility was to plan and be prepared to conduct the defense of South Korea in my area, which included approximately 50% of the country's population as well as its financial, light industrial, and main governmental areas," Vaught said.

Approximately 90% of the soldiers under his command were South Korean.

"Why not a Korean commander?" Vaught asked. "There are many Korean generals who are quite capable of doing the job, but it is considered significantly important by the South Koreans to have a senior American authority on the ground who would be involved early in any renewal of hostilities that North Korea might initiate."

Vaught's day-to-day activities included planning for the defense and participating in the planning for various, frequent exercises, both scheduled and unscheduled, to be sure the forces were always ready to make a best effort to contend with any actions on the part of North Korea.

"I spent a lot of time out in the field working with my subordinate commanders," Vaught said. "I talked with my corps commanders frequently to make sure we all understood the war plan and that we had a very good comprehension of what to expect in the early days, if the enemy renewed hostilities."

Vaught said he believed the most critical time would be in the first 8-15 days of renewed hostilities because the United States would be very limited in its ability to reinforce during that period.

"The first critical phase of the war will occur before the U.S. can bring dominant combat power to the area," Vaught said. "We have some tactical air power there and the possibility of bringing in additional air power, depending on where the American carrier groups are located. The planning and use of tactical air power is very important because it would be used to frustrate and stop any attack by the North Koreans."

In Vaught's judgment, the South Koreans possess some of the best light infantry units in the world. Vaught said some U.S. ground forces would be involved in hostilities, but the main U.S. contributions in the early days would be tactical air and logistics support.

When he arrived in September 1981, an immediate challenge Vaught faced was the war plan itself.

"Essentially, it said we're going to hold for a while on line A, then we'll fall back to line B, then line C, and ultimately line D, which was on the outskirts of Seoul," Vaught said. "By that time, we'll be so desperate we'll figure out what to do next. It was not a very satisfactory concept of defense."

With the consent of General John Wickham, Commander in Chief of the United Nations Command Korea, Vaught began considering some alternate plans. A "dynamic defense" plan was developed with the concept of holding a successful defense as far north of Seoul as possible in the first 8-15 days. As soon as the North Korean offensive could be slowed down or stopped, a striking corps reserve would be formed that would take the offensive and strike back to the north.

"In other words, we would conduct a defense for the classic reason that a defense is always conducted, to buy time and to position to enable you to go over to the offensive," Vaught said. "The Koreans understood and agreed with that."

A "minute man concept" was developed for the five South Korean ready reserve divisions that would be called to duty immediately upon any North Korean attack. The equipment for these divisions was readily available in the reserve area with weapons stored at police stations. When notified of an attack by radio and police channels, soldiers of these divisions would immediately go to their forward defensive position rather than wasting time going through reactivation processing in some other area. Using this concept, within 24-48 hours of the initial attack, five more divisions would be in the field to back up the front-line divisions. In this way, the regular structure divisions could be formed into a corps to initiate a counterattack.

"With careful arranging of the plan throughout the combined field army area, we had a very soundly conceived, high-confidence defense plan that the Koreans had a lot of confidence in," Vaught said.

Vaught routinely met with his commanders in the field down to the brigade command. Each of the commanders would specifically describe his defense plan, including the likelihood of enemy penetration from various directions and what could be done to block that.

"Thereby, we had a very thorough concept of how to use combined arms teams, and I felt very confident that down to at least brigade level, my commanders knew what was expected of them," Vaught said. "I emphasized that they were going to have to stay out there and fight for hours and days, maybe even as long as a week without a lot of critique and review from higher headquarters."

"I personally believe that the early days of a renewed conflict will be so chaotic and in such high-intensity type of ground and air warfare that we can't fully contemplate the situation that is going to confront us," Vaught said. "It's going to require a lot of determined effort by the armed forces of South Korea and the South Korean government to maintain some modicum of control until the situation begins to clarify itself."

Vaught believed one way to solidify the actions of the South Koreans and to give a shot in the arm to South Korean morale was to get on the offensive as soon as possible.

"Our plan and concept would enable that reality and was a plan that was very attractive to the South Koreans," Vaught said. "The South Koreans understand you can't win a fight without going on the offensive, and they do not want to sacrifice the city of Seoul because the effectiveness of any government that sacrifices Seoul without determined resistance would be questioned."

Vaught said the weather and the successes or failures of the North Koreans and their use of air power would be factors in any new conflict, but the outcome will largely count on the determination of the Combined Forces Command and the effectiveness of its planning to take on the enemy. Virtually the entire North Korean army is disposed near the DMZ. It has armor and dug-in artillery that can shell all the forward positions. The North Koreans have the ability to initiate war in a period where we would have no more than twelve hours warning.

"The only hope of holding Seoul and keeping the enemy from getting there and burning and plundering that city is to get on the offensive quickly and take the fight back to them," Vaught said. "That's what the dynamic defense is designed to do."

The Korean situation is interesting in that during the early days of the Carter administration, some decisions were made to withdraw U.S. troops from South Korea. Some were actually withdrawn, and more were scheduled for withdrawal until reconsideration of the enemy threat and other factors caused the next withdrawal to be cancelled. These actions on the part of the U.S. administration suggested to the South Koreans they should become more self-sufficient.

Accordingly, the South Korean government went to considerable expense to develop a national program for increasing war material production. A defense industries complex, called the Chang Won Defense Industrial Complex, was developed in the southern end of South Korea. With a number of modern factories, it was capable of turning out much of the equipment the armed forces needed to conduct a sustained battle with North Korea. Shortening logistic lines to just South Korea—rather than extended ones to Japan, Guam, or the western United States—makes it that much more likely that South Korea can survive an attack from North Korea.

"With twice the population of North Korea and a larger and much more modern industrial base than the North, I believe South Korea has many reasons to suspect it would win any renewed conflict," Vaught said.

Commanding an army in a foreign country where a very large number of the troops are natives of that country could lead to problems if not handled correctly. Vaught said he didn't feel any resentment by the South Koreans of his position nor any resentment based on nationalistic feelings.

Reflecting on his command of the Combined Field Army, Vaught said, "I had total cooperation and I believe respect, based upon the anticipation that I would be an effective commander and, indeed, their trust would be well placed in me to do those things that were necessary to defend their country."

Lieutenant General Vaught presents an award at Camp Red Cloud, South Korea in Jan 1982

Chapter Twenty

Vaught retired in January 1983 after nearly thirty-eight years of continuous service on active duty with the U.S. Army. His career began as a draftee and ended as a three-star general, something which is exceedingly rare in Army circles, especially considering his commission was obtained through the Officer's Candidate School and not a service academy or Reserve Officer's Training Corps program.

After retirement, Vaught was asked what advice he had for young officers just beginning their career.

"Be yourself, tell the truth, level with your soldiers, follow the Golden Rule and the rules of a prudent man," he responded. "Do what's right for your country, do what's right for your soldiers, be selfless about your service, and put duty first."

"Duty is the most sublime word in the English language," Vaught continued. "I'll always believe that to the bottom of my being. It was a great honor to serve our country."

Those are the words of a true patriot and a true gentleman. Vaught was the best example of both.

After Vaught's retirement from the Army in 1983, he tended to downplay his retirement years, but they were filled with a continuing interest in national defense, world affairs, and local issues.

"Being retired, the opportunities to render effective and useful service aren't very numerous," he said. "Other than talking to various civilian forums, at one time or another, or working as a consultant, one doesn't have an opportunity to contribute in the same direct ways that I was fortunate enough to have afforded to me while I was in positions of responsibility in the U.S. Army."

Some of the highlights of his retirement years include the following:

Vaught was a consultant and adviser to military and civilian agencies in the development and production of avionics, digital communications, night vision equipment, and radar for military use, such as special operations.

He was a member of the special operations policy and advisory group for the Office of the Secretary of Defense.

In 1985, Vaught chaired a study group sponsored by the American Security Council. The group produced and sent the "Peace through Strength" proposal to the White House. President Ronald Reagan adopted the idea and used it to neutralize and eliminate the Soviet Union without firing a shot.

Vaught was in Seoul, South Korea, when the North Koreans announced they had violated the 1994 "No Nuclear Weapons in Korea" agreement, which prompted him to write the "Six Nations" proposal. Vaught sent the proposal to all six capitals – the United States, China, Japan, North Korea, Russia, and South Korea – and implored them to use diplomacy to stop North Korea's nuclear weapons program.

In March 2006, Vaught received the National Defense Industrial Association's Special Operations/Low Intensity Conflict Lifetime Achievement Award for his more than sixty years of contributions to the U.S. Special Operations Community.

Throughout his retirement, Vaught continued to author "White Papers" on various positions regarding national defense, international affairs, and other government issues. His reading and research were voluminous, and the final products always found their way to top advisers to whichever administration was in office at the time.

Vaught didn't prefer one political party over another, but he was quick to offer advice on issues of which he was knowledgeable to whoever was in power at the time and thoughtful criticism when he felt it was warranted.

Vaught returned to live full-time in his native Horry County, South Carolina in the mid-1990s. Almost immediately, he took an interest in local affairs. The county was growing rapidly, and issues such as zoning, inter-connectability of roads, and quality of life quickly grabbed his interest.

Vaught was a constant attendee of Horry County Council and Horry County Planning and Zoning Committee meetings, often speaking on specific issues. His presentations were plain talk, honest, forthright expressions of his views on a particular subject, often punctuated with the expression "Get it done."

He will long be remembered for his advocacy for International Drive, a connecting road between a rapidly growing area of Horry County and an internal county road providing north/south access. It was needed for many reasons but was held up by governmental "red tape," both state and local, for a number of years. Nevertheless, Vaught continued his one-man crusade to get the road built, finally having it included in a list of road projects that would be paid by a special one-cent capital projects sales tax.

In July 2018, the Horry County Council rewarded Vaught's legacy as well as his involvement with local issues by renaming International Drive the "Lieutenant General James B. Vaught Memorial Highway."

In his later years, Vaught was troubled by some heart issues as well as the effects of injuries he sustained while on active duty. However, he maintained his driving spirit and was always involved in one project or another.

Vaught died September 20, 2013, by falling out of a boat and drowning. However, Horry County Coroner Robert Edge noted signs of heart disease, and there was speculation Vaught suffered a heart attack prior to falling from the boat.

His funeral was attended by national, state, and local dignitaries as well as family and friends from Horry County. While there was a large contingent of retired brass in attendance, an impressive number of former enlisted men came to pay their respects to Vaught's memory. Troopers from the 5th of the 7th, Red Hats from the Vietnamese Paratroopers, members of the hostage task force, and individuals from other duty locations in Vaught's career all made the trip because Vaught had touched their lives in a positive manner.

There is a lot to be said about a retired general to whose funeral enlisted men who served under him take the time and make the effort to be a part of the remembrance. Lieutenant General James B. Vaught was truly a positive leader of men.

Vaught at the 30th Anniversary Iran Hostage Rescue Memorial Event in 2010

Epilogue
A Conversation with Florence Vaught – July 14, 2018

"He was the most lovable old gruff general you ever wanted to meet."
– Florence Vaught

Florence and Jim Vaught first met as students at Conway (SC) High School in the early 1940s. Their first contact was Jim tutoring Florence for a Geometry test they were both scheduled to take. Florence got an A on the test, while James got a B.

"When I got an A and Jim got a B, Jim got mad," Florence said.

But he didn't stay mad for long. Throughout their final two years together at Conway High School, Florence and Jim sat together in classes in which they were both enrolled. Student theater productions also provided time together as Florence was an actress and Jim built sets for the plays. As football captain, Jim got to choose the members of the cheerleading squad, and Florence was a cheerleader.

However, they never had a formal date because they lived miles apart in rural South Carolina and Jim did not have a car.

"To have a boyfriend you never dated was strange, but there was a chemistry there," Florence said. "The only times we were together was at football practices and play practices."

Being one year ahead of Florence in school, Jim went off to the Citadel while Florence was a senior in high school.

"He invited me to a dance at the Citadel, but my mother said I was not old enough to go there alone," Florence said.

When Jim got drafted into the Army halfway through his sophomore year at the Citadel, it seemed their relationship was at an end. Florence got engaged while Jim was stationed in Germany, and they did not connect personally again for over fifty years. The drama coach at Conway High School, Florence Epps, was a mentor to both and kept them informed about each other throughout that 50-year interval even though they were both married to other people.

Florence's husband of forty-eight years died in 1994. In February 1995, she received a call from Jim.

"I answered the phone and he said, 'Florence, this is Tiger' (a nickname from his high school football days). We talked for a long time, and we talked every few weeks until we went out to dinner in the summer of 1995."

That dinner was the first time they had met in person since Florence was a senior in high school.

"There was still a chemistry there, but I denied it for a while," Florence said. "Before he left me that night Jim said, 'I never stopped loving you.'"

On April 12, 1997, Jim and Florence got married. They lived an incredibly close and happy life together until Jim died in September 2013.

"He had a very soft side to him," Florence said. "He was always helping people in need, but then there was the gruff side that came from his years in the Army."

The Vaughts did a lot of traveling in their sixteen years together, especially on river cruises. They visited a number of countries several times including Russia, Finland, Ukraine, the Czech Republic, Slovakia, and Hungary. They also traveled to

Seoul, South Korea a number of times, visiting South Korean officials Jim had first met in his last tour of duty in the Army.

"My favorite trip was when we traveled on the Trans-Siberian Railroad," Florence said. "The trip took eight days, went through seven time zones, and nobody else on the train spoke English. It was quite an experience."

Shortly after they were married, Jim and Florence Vaught came back to live in Horry County, South Carolina, just outside of Conway where it all began for the two of them.

"I always said I would never go back to Conway to live, but here I am," Florence said.

Florence has a hallway in her house that she calls "The Museum" complete with an official portrait of Jim as a Lieutenant General, a display case containing the many medals he was awarded during his Army career, and many other plaques and mementoes of his career.

While they were not together during his 38-year career in the Army, Florence has a deep understanding of what Jim did for the country. She got to meet many of his peers from those years at conferences and social occasions that are part of the life of retired generals.

"We went to Fort Myer, Virginia the day after September 11, 2001. Immediately after we checked into the hotel, Jim went to the Pentagon. I didn't see him again for three days. When he got back to the hotel, Jim was very unhappy about the base not being safe enough," Florence said.

"To prove a point, he took a book he had brought for the Chief of Staff of the Army over to his quarters at night. He snuck around the guards and left the book on the front porch. The next morning, he called the general and told him he ought to be happy the book Jim left by his front door was not a bomb. That was the gruff general," Florence said.

More importantly, she got to be married for sixteen years to a man who loved her for a lifetime.

"He was always bringing flowers and cards home for me," Florence said. "He told me many times 'I would be lost without my wife.' I got to see his romantic side and also the gruff general that I never really knew. He was a most wonderful man."

GEOMETRY CLASS

William Rutledge	Joe Hughes
Martin Kahn	Phil Edwards
Frances Woodle	Barry Gause
Betty Henderson	Henry Watson
Betty Ford	Robert Hamilton
Claire Goldfinch	Albert Long
Mozelle Floyd	Willis Duncan
Ruth Magrath	James Vaught
Dorothy Proctor	Mary Katherine Nye
Burrous Huggins	Billy Duncan
Robert Green	Florence Robinson
Billy Watson	D. K. Stalvey
Hobson Hucks	Jimmie Henderson
Myron Hodges	

Teacher . . . . . . Mrs. Ford

Conway High School (Conway, SC) in 1943

Jim, Florence, and Joshua Vaught in 2011

Funeral Speech by Captain Bryan Vaught, USMCR

September 28, 2013

Good Afternoon. Being the grandson of Lieutenant General Jim Vaught has definitely had its share of benefits. For starters, I was one of the few people who never had to call him "Sir" but rather had the privilege of calling him "Grandpa." So today, rather than elaborate on his long and distinguished military career, I will talk about my personal experiences with him and share a few stories that perhaps you've never heard.

The lighter side of "Grim Jim" was a kinder, more loving man that few people outside of his family ever witnessed. The first time I really remembered meeting my Grandpa was when I was about seven years old. We were living in Fayetteville, North Carolina at the time, and Grandpa Jim would often travel to Fort Bragg on business trips, having just recently retired from the Army a few years earlier. As a kid, you tend to remember special times and events that are outside the norm, and a surprise visit from a Grandpa who happened to be in town was definitely one of those times.

Soon after Grandpa arrived, he picked up my sister Megan and I and asked us where *we* would like to eat for dinner. Well, I had never felt so much power and decision-making authority in my life—that I, being only seven, got to choose where we went for dinner, and it wasn't even my birthday. "Chuck E. Cheese!" Well, it was called Showbiz Pizza back then, but it was all the same to me and Megan—pizza, video games, and air hockey with Grandpa, and then we each got to pick a prize before we left. I remember having a crush on a girl in my second-grade class, and so I decided to spend my hundred tickets on a gold-colored plastic ring with a large fake gemstone. Grandpa Jim grinned and found my choice prizes amusing. Before he dropped us off back at our house, I remember him telling us to be good and obey our Mom, and then he talked about how much he enjoyed spending time with us. Then, before I left the car, he would say, "Bryan, now put this in your pocket." Wow, a five-dollar-bill! It might as well have been a million dollars to a seven-year-old. Megan and I absolutely loved his special evening visits, and these were some of the best times that I remember having as a kid.

During my summers as a teenager, I spent many days visiting with my Grandpa. Now you may not have ever had the pleasure of riding on it, but Grandpa Jim once had a boat. Not a nice boat that was well maintained, but a boat more fitting of his personality—several years old, rugged, and it often smelled like pluff mud. He would take us out on that boat to go tubing, and he would keep driving figure eights faster and faster on the river until we flew off the innertube. However, on more than one occasion, that old boat's engine would seize up and we would be stuck out in the middle of the Charleston River somewhere miles from anyone else. Oh, and of course this was well before we had cell phones to call for help. Fortunately, Grandpa kept an old bag of tools, a "bottle of WD" (he vowed that you could fix almost anything with WD-40), and a rusted can of engine starting fluid. He and my Dad would tenaciously repair that old motor until it finally sputtered back to life, after what seemed like the better part of the afternoon. We always somehow made it back to the marina because my Grandpa had a special trait, which I grew to admire—his stubborn optimism.

Perhaps it was his years of formal education, extensive leadership training, or seasoned experience gained on the battlefield of three major wars, but I personally feel that his can-do spirit was forged during his childhood growing up on a farm during the 1930s-era Great Depression. He reminded me that **"There are three types of people in this world: Those that make things happen, those who stand around and watch other people make things happen, and those who don't know what the hell is happening."** It was quite obvious that he preferred the first type of individual, and he personified that work ethic to the maximum extent in his daily life. Grandpa Jim didn't actually retire in the traditional sense, when you play golf all the time, sit around the house, and host weekend garden parties. Even in his mid-80s, he still continued writing strategy letters to Presidents Bush and Obama that impacted current events across the globe, he started a new Veteran's Association, and he influenced several local construction and community projects throughout South Carolina.

Even though Grandpa may have been guilty of having "too many irons in the fire" to the average person, I personally believe that his projects gave him hope and a sense of purpose to continue living to see them through to completion. Whenever one project would reach a temporary standstill, he always seemed to have five others to fall back on. His stubborn optimism helped him to eventually succeed and find innovative ways to get things done that nobody else had considered. Grandpa once told me a story about how he was frequently the go-to guy in the Army when a mission needed to be accomplished. "Give it to Vaught, he'll get it done!" the Commander would say, and miraculously he nearly always came through in the end.

Well, even though my Grandpa has physically passed away, he's really still here with us. Right now, I'm certain that he's up in Heaven, but somehow able to influence life events here on Earth (in spirit). General Douglas MacArthur once said that "Old Soldiers never die, they just fade away." Well, if that adage is true, then my Grandpa's legacy will keep shining on for many years to come. General Vaught will continue his service somehow; in fact, I'm sure that God has wasted little time with pleasantries, and by now he has already tasked him with some important projects to work on. Fortunately, since it's Heaven, perhaps everything will finally go *exactly the way that Jim* planned it. May God bless you all for coming to my Grandpa's funeral, and I suspect that Jim Vaught is up there grinning down on us right now, and so grateful that we are here remembering him today. Thank you.

2nd Lieutenant Bryan Vaught, USMC and Lieutenant General Jim Vaught, USA Ret.
Quantico, VA in October 2003

Operation Eagle Claw Paintings

Outside The White House in 1981

Camp Red Cloud, South Korea 1981-1983

Retirement Years 1990's

Retirement Years 2000-2003

Retirement Years 2004-2008

Retirement Years 2009-2011

Retirement Years 2012-2013

Gone, but never forgotten...

About the Authors

Paul served ten years on active duty with the U. S. Naval Security Group Command from October 6, 1970 until October 29, 1980. He moved to Horry County, South Carolina in September 1983 and worked as a journalist concentrating on local and state political issues as well as writing a weekly Veteran profile. Paul first met General Vaught when he served as a member of the Horry County Solid Waste Authority Board of Directors in the late 1990s. Paul currently writes for the Grand Strand Daily Website.

Paul Gable and his late wife Kathy

Major Bryan Vaught is the son of James B. Vaught, Jr. and grandson of Lieutenant General Jim Vaught. He graduated from The Citadel in 2002 and has served in the Marine Corps for the past sixteen years, including a MEU deployment to the Pacific, a combat tour in Iraq, and service with Marine Corps Special Operations Command (MARSOC). He has written and published multiple articles and white papers for the *Marine Corps Gazette* and Defense Advanced Research Projects Agency (DARPA). He currently serves at Marine Forces Reserve Headquarters in New Orleans.

Bryan Vaught and his wife Debra

Made in the USA
Coppell, TX
19 May 2021